Bonny Bhattacharjee

Older Adults and Computers

Bonny Bhattacharjee

Older Adults and Computers

An Insight into a Complex Relationship

VDM Verlag Dr. Müller

Imprint

Bibliographic information by the German National Library: The German National Library lists this publication at the German National Bibliography; detailed bibliographic information is available on the Internet at http://dnb.d-nb.de.

Any brand names and product names mentioned in this book are subject to trademark, brand or patent protection and are trademarks or registered trademarks of their respective holders. The use of brand names, product names, common names, trade names, product descriptions etc. even without a particular marking in this works is in no way to be construed to mean that such names may be regarded as unrestricted in respect of trademark and brand protection legislation and could thus be used by anyone.

Cover image: www.purestockx.com

Publisher:
VDM Verlag Dr. Müller Aktiengesellschaft & Co. KG , Dudweiler Landstr. 125 a, 66123 Saarbrücken, Germany,
Phone +49 681 9100-698, Fax +49 681 9100-988,
Email: info@vdm-verlag.de

Zugl.: Tallahassee, Florida State University, Diss., 2007

Produced in USA and UK by:
Lightning Source Inc., La Vergne, Tennessee, USA
Lightning Source UK Ltd., Milton Keynes, UK
BookSurge LLC, 5341 Dorchester Road, Suite 16, North Charleston, SC 29418, USA

ISBN: 978-3-639-06876-4

The present research is dedicated to Professor
Dr. Corinne Jorgensen, without her selfless effort this
dissertation would never have been a reality. Dr. Jorgensen
guided the author of the present study as a mentor, in
surmounting innumerable barriers, which came up all along,
since the dissertation-writing phase commenced. She
literally taught the researcher to traverse the difficult
domain of academia. Mere words can't express what she has
done for the author of this study. The author of this
research shall forever be grateful to this magnanimous
personality.

ACKNOWLEDGEMENTS

I am truly grateful all my committee members and
Dr. Barbara Palmer for agreeing to join my committee.

I am also grateful to Mr. Steven Brown and
Dr. Mahtab Marker from the Department of Statistics, for
providing all the help needed in coming up with a feasible
study design.

Also, I am deeply indebted to Dr. Julie Thomas, for
supplying me with the mechanism for coding the Computer
Anxiety Scale (CAS; Cohen & Waugh, 1989).

I am also grateful to Ms. Carrie Norton, for
consenting to help with the distribution of questionnaires
and informed consent forms among the potential participants
of the study.

TABLE OF CONTENTS

LIST OF TABLES

vi

vii

LIST OF FIGURES

ABSTRACT

The purpose of the present study lay in considering
and providing accurate descriptions of the factors known to
encourage or alternatively discourage computer usage among
older employees within an academic setting.

Primarily, the two independent variables of the study
are *age-related-infirmity* (*W/WT*), and *computer-anxiety*. The
dependent variable of the study is *barriers-to-computer-
use*. The literature review reveals that *age-related -
infirmity* (*W/WT*), a variable with two levels *with age-
related infirmity* and *without age-related-infirmity*
represents impairments which come with old age and which
are known to intervene with the possibility of a smooth
computer interaction, for older users. *Computer-anxiety*,
the other independent variable, is known as a common
emotional response to computers.

A review of the literature demonstrated that the
predictor variable of the independent variable *age-related-
infirmity* (*W/WT*) is *age*, and the predictor variables of the
independent variables *computer-anxiety* are: *age* (positive
or direct linear relationship) *gender* - represented at two
levels; *male* (positive or direct linear relationship),
female (negative or inverse linear relationship); *income*
(negative or inverse linear relationship); *education*
(negative or inverse linear relationship); *computer -
ownership* represented at two levels *owner* (negative or
inverse relationship) and *non-owner* (positive or direct
linear relationship); (computer) *experience* (negative or
inverse linear relationship); and the dichotomous variable
disability -represented at two levels *disabled* (direct

linear or positive relationship) and *not-disabled* (negative or inverse linear relationship).

The research dealt with an important user group, the older adult users of computer technology. What makes the older adults an important subsection of the United States' population, and the subject matter of studies such as this one, are their expanding numbers and their growing economic strength. Despite this, however, the chasm between the older adults and information technologies continues to bother experts. The author of the study believes that technological backwardness of older adults can only harm their interests and make them vulnerable to societal discrimination and subject them to perpetual backwardness. Thus the need of the hour should be about focusing on the factors and forces which affect the possibilities of a digital divide among the potential older users of computer technology, with the ultimate aim of weeding these forces out totally. This is what this study intends to do.

The research sought answers to the following questions: whether there is a dichotomous relationship between the predictor variable *gender* (*M/F*) and the variable *computer-anxiety;* whether there is a relationship between the variable *computer-anxiety*, and each of the demographic variables (on a separate basis), *income*, *education*, and (computer) *experience;* whether the dichotomous variable *computer-ownership* (*O/NO*) has a two-fold relationship with the variable *computer-anxiety;* whether the demographic variable *age* affects the variable *computer-anxiety* in a direct fashion. The first hypothesis stated that the variable *age* has a two-fold relationship with the variable *age-related-infirmity* (*W/WT*). The second hypothesis stated that there is a direct linear

relationship between the variable *computer-anxiety* and the
variable *barriers-to-computer-use*, and the third hypothesis
assumed that the variable *age-related-infirmity* (*W/WT*) has
a two-fold relationship with the dependent variable
barriers-to-computer-use.

The data for the study was collected through the use
of a survey questionnaires modified from previous studies;
a survey questionnaire devised by the author herself in the
aftermath of reviewing the literature; and a demographic
questionnaire. The study employed a stratified random
sampling technique in selecting the study's sample who were
Florida State University's (FSU) permanent employees in the
age group of 55 years or older. Statistical analysis was
conducted using SPSS. Data analysis revealed that for this
population, the variable *gender* (*M/F*) does not have an
effect on the variable *computer-anxiety*; it demonstrated a
statistically significant negative or inverse linear
relationship between the variables *income* and *computer-anxiety*;
no significant relationship was found to exist
between the variables *education* and *computer-anxiety*;
analysis proved that there is a negative or inverse linear
relationship between the variables (computer) *experience*
and *computer-anxiety*; the variable *computer-ownership* (*NO*)
was found to have a direct linear or positive relationship
with the variable *computer-anxiety*, and the variable
computer-ownership (*O*) was found to have an inverse linear
or negative relationship with the variable *computer-anxiety*;
the variable *disability* (*D/ND*) was not found to
have any relationship with the variable *computer-anxiety*;
and also the variable *age* was not found to be correlated
with the variable *computer-anxiety*. However, the study was
successful in establishing the fact that the variable

computer-anxiety is positively related (implying a direct linear relationship) to the independent variable *barriers-to-computer-use*, although it failed to prove that the other independent variable *age-related-infirmity* (*W/WT*) has any relationship with the study's outcome variable *barriers-to-computer-use*.

Any future research should replicate the study among people of varying backgrounds and employment status. The study's significance lay in endorsing the precise nature of relationships which literature review confirms as being in existence between each of the predictor variables *income*, (computer) *experience*, and *computer ownership* (*O/NO*), and the response variable *computer-anxiety*. At the same time the study's results were successful in proving that computer-anxiety is a barrier factor for computer technology access. This is quite important if we keep in mind the fact that the data for the study was gathered from a relatively well-off and an atypical older adult population; who differed considerably from the general older adults, in terms of their income and education.

INTRODUCTION

The present study was undertaken from a need to evaluate the impact of two major factors which have been identified as creating barriers to computer use and access among senior computer users. These factors are: 1.*Age-related-infirmity;* and 2. *Computer-anxiety.*

1. *Age-related-infirmity (W/WT)*: This factor envisages a host of infirmities, which accompany old age, which include decrement in seniors' memory structures, vision, musculo-skeletal systems, etc. These infirmities have been identified as major sources of barriers, keeping older adults from effectively adapting to a culture spawned by the technology of computers.

For example, memory impairments among the elderly reduce their ability to build conceptual models of the functioning of the interface, as the activity relies on remembering sequences of action and reasoning among them, thereby hindering their abilities to retrace and navigate a web-based route. Also, older adults' age-related visual impairments make it difficult for them to view standard screens designed for the normal users. Therefore *age-related-infirmity (W/WT)* has been identified as a factor preventing older adults from using computer technology in an optimal fashion, both in terms of frequency and intensity. The variable *age* has been identified as the chief predictor variable for *age-related-infirmity (W/WT)*, and the latter's relationship with the variable *age* was explored during the course of this research (Kurniawan & Zaphiris; Worden, Walker & Bharat, 1997; Czaja, 2007; Whitcomb, 2007).

1

The literature review revealed that significant association/relationship exists between the demographic variable *age* and the dichotomous variable *age-related-infirmity* represented at two levels as people (i) *with age-related-infirmity*, and people (ii) *without age-related-infirmity (W/WT)*.

2. *Computer-anxiety*: Known to be a psycho-physiological construct that manifests in users as fear of impending interaction with computers, which is disproportionate to the actual threat posed by the technology; this leads to decreased computer use and avoidance of computers on the part of the users (Doyle, Stamouli, & Huggard, 2005; Howard, Murphy & Thomas, 1986; Orr, 2007).

In an effort to know more about computer-anxiety, the author conducted an intensive literature review of the underlying variables which are known to influence the psychological construct – computer-anxiety. It was found that significant associations exist between each of the following socio-economic-demographic predictor variables: *age*; *gender* represented at two levels (i) *male* (ii) *female* (*M/F*); *income*; *education*; *computer-ownership* represented at two levels (i) *owner*, (ii) *non-owner* (*O/NO*); (computer) *experience*; *disability* represented at two levels (i) *disabled* (ii) *not-disabled* (*D/ND*); and their outcome variable *computer-anxiety*.

The author conducted the study in two stages; in the first stage she highlighted and focused on the underlying factors which are known to impact/influence the major barrier causing variables associated with computer use, *age-related-infirmity (W/WT)*, and *computer-anxiety*, with an intention to determine whether or not these underlying

2

factors correlate/associate with their respective outcome variables.

In the second stage the researcher analyzed the causal relationship/ association between the two hitherto mentioned barrier causing variables - *age-related-infirmity* (*W/WT*) and *computer-anxiety* -and the final response variable of the study *barriers-to-computer-use*.

Within the scope of this study, the socio-economic-and demographic variables which have been demonstrated to have a causal relationship/association with the dichotomous variable *age-related-infirmity* (*W/WT*) and *computer-anxiety*, were referred to as the underlying independent variables.

Age-related-infirmity (*W/WT*) and *computer-anxiety*, also an independent variable of this study, were vetted separately for the nature of their associations, with the final outcome variable *barriers-to-computer-use*.

The research dealt with an important user group, the older adult users of computer technology. What makes the older adults an important subsection of the United States' population, and the subject matter of studies such as this one, are their expanding numbers and their growing economic strength. Baldi (1997) concludes that the older adults are the fastest growing section of the population in the United States. Rubin and White-Means (2000) contend that the economic prowess of this segment of the population has been increasing steadily and the relative well being of older adults in comparison to the rest of the population is now an established fact.

Despite this, however, the chasm between older adults and information technologies continues to bother experts. Charness and Holley (2004) dwell on the aspect of

3

technological impoverishment of this section of the population, by endorsing the possibility of "a real 'digital divide' as a function of age" (p.418).

Technological poverty among the old can be scary, and may have several economic implications for the old and for society in general. A major positive impact of information technologies, under the present economic set-up, is in the domain of job restructuring and job configuration. A worker's skill in fulfilling certain aspects of technology-driven job processes is thus a requirement for the workforce of today (Borghans & Weel, 2002; Hoffman, 2006).

However, in the backdrop of this high-technology and high-skill employment scenario, older adults are finding themselves increasingly relegated to the backburner. More and more of them are falling prey to managerial biases, and are being labeled as too inflexible and too difficult to train, and hence unsuitable for unemployment (Randall, 2006; Bartel & Sicherman, 1993; Samorodov, 1999).

Hartley, Hartley, & Johnson (1996) are of the opinion that older adults tend to find themselves outside of a technology-powered employment scenario mainly because of managements' impression that computer technology is not for the old but for the "yuppies" and the "techno-geeks" only.

In the IT (Information Technology) sector itself older adults face biases in employability prospects. Evans (1999) is of the opinion that the very nature of IT (Information Technology) jobs, which call for familiarity with the latest computer driven technologies, tends to militate against older adults' possibilities of getting a job in the sector.

Studies affirm that indeed computer use among the older workforce tends to decline due to reasons like older

4

workers' natural inability to adapt to the technology of computers, and from a sense of apathy among elders in the workforce about investing in computer skills when they are so close to retirement (Friedberg, 2001).

The author of the present study thinks that the gap between older adults and computer technology, besides costing the older adults their jobs, has the potential of eventually leading them to a situation where industries and businesses in a knowledge based, innovative economic set-up, would have to do without the labor power of an otherwise experienced and dependable work force, which is undergoing an increasing span of work life (Steinhauser, 2006; Pennar, Perun & Steuerle, 2003; Van Leeuwe, 2006). Also, the possibility of leaving out the elderly of the country's population from the information technology loop can also come at a huge ethical cost (Carpenter, 2006; Finn, 2006).

This is especially true in a society where information technology is becoming integral to work, education, and general quality of life. Also, in present day information societies, technologies are found to be the factor behind peoples overall standing in a highly stratified society. For example, studies have shown that employees of a large firm differed perceptibly in their knowledge about their organization, depending on whether or not they used network enabled computers. Also it was found that 63% of the adults who used network enabled computers scored high on quizzes based on current events, compared to those without network access (Bikson & Panis, 1995).

Finn (2006) believes that our society is ethically obligated to seek the integration of the technologically disadvantaged seniors by trying to address their computer-related concerns.

The author believes that the technological backwardness of older adults can only harm their interests and make them vulnerable to societal discrimination and subject them to perpetual backwardness. Thus the need of the hour is about focusing on the factors and forces which are affecting the possibilities of a digital divide among the potential older users of computer technology, with an ultimate aim of weeding these forces out totally. This is exactly what this study intends to do.

There is a considerable amount of ambiguity woven around the term "older adults." In the absence of a general consensus about what the term actually means, older adults as a category may have different connotations for different people. For example, the AARP (American Association for Retired People) uses the term older adult to mean people of or over the age of 50 years ("Microsoft, AARP Announce Alliance To Provide Technology Springboard for Older Americans," 1997). The American Psychological Association (APA) on the other hand, considers the age 65 years as a cut-off point for one to qualify as an older adult (Cooley et al.; 1997).

The Department of Elder Affairs- State of Florida (DOEA), however, considers people of or over the age of 55 years as older adults. In a joint communiqué published with the Agency for Workforce Innovation (AWI), on the occasion of Older Worker Week, the agency clearly articulates its practice of identifying that part of the workforce as seniors which consists of workers who are 55 years of age and above ("Elder Affairs and Agency for Workforce Innovation Praise Older Workers," 2005). Since the present

6

study, was conducted in the state of Florida, we decided to abide by this definition of the term older adult, by slotting people of or over the age of 55- years into the older adult category.

The study was conducted on the main campus of Florida State University (FSU). The subjects for the study were chosen through a sampling procedure from among Florida State University's older adult teaching and non-teaching permanent employee population. A set of three questionnaires was administered to the selected individuals, with a view to determining how the variables *age*, *gender(M/F)*, *income*, *education*, *computer ownership(O/NO)*, (computer) *experience*, *disability(D/ND)* status etc., relate to the phenomena of *age-related-infirmity(W/WT)* and *computer-anxiety*, two known barrier factors in computer technology access for the older users.

Florida State University

With its main campus situated in Tallahassee, Florida, the FSU is a public institution of higher education having a student body of nearly 40,000. Something unique about the university is its distinction as one of the most wired colleges/universities of United States America (Torralba, 2000; "Office of Institutional Research," 2006).

The potential of FSU as a wired institution of higher learning made its selection as a context for execution of the present study, a worthwhile fact. By executing this study in such a unique backdrop, the researcher sought to determine whether the same factors which either positively or negatively influence the potential of a successful bonding between older users and computers retain their effects among a relatively well-heeled older user

7

population represented by FSU's senior permanent employee
population.

Statement of the Problem

The research sought to determine the manner in which
socio-economic and demographic variables, such as *age*,
gender, *income*, *education*, *computer-ownership* (*O/NO*),
(computer) *experience*, and *disability* (*D/ND*) status of
older users condition computer technology use, indirectly
by affecting *age-related-infirmity* (*W/WT*) and *computer-
anxiety*, and in turn how the two barrier factors associate
with the variable *barrier-to-computer-use* in aggravating or
alternatively easing resistance towards computer use among
older adult users of the technology.

The uniqueness of the study lay in its socio-
biological orientation (borne out by the nature of the
variables under study), and in its purpose to study older
adults' use of computer technology from a wide socio-
economic and human-factors' perspective, using a primarily
sociological methodological approach.

Also, very few studies have presented a view from
bottom-up, within a mix of older users' socio-economic and
physio-mental characteristics, with a view to discerning
how their presence affects the senior user population's
interaction with computer technology. This mindset finds
affirmation in the claims made by authors like Bethea
(2002), who states that little communication research has
been conducted, so far, around the issue of older adults'
barriers to accessing technologies. This stance is
supported by additional research studies which affirm the
issue of older adults' barriers to technology has not been
adequately addressed from such perspectives as the needs,
wants, and preferences of older users, their experiences

8

and attitudes towards technology, their education, finances and general standard of living, and how the issue of barriers to access computer technology fit into the scenario (Eisma, et al., 2003).

The trend does speak volumes about an effort on the part of scholars and researchers towards bringing older adults into the sphere of an information driven socio-economic structure, through increased research on factors and variables which are known to affect the computing patterns of older users. The present study promises to build upon the bases established by such studies.

Purpose of the Study

The purpose of the present study lay in considering, evaluating and providing accurate descriptions of the factors known even to remotely encourage and alternatively discourage computer usage among older people.

By relating independent variable *age-related-infirmity* *(W/WT)*, with its underlying predictor variable *age* in a causal manner, the researcher tried to determine whether there is a positive correlation between the variable *age* and *age-related-infirmity* *(W/WT)*.

The study also assessed the extent and nature of association between a wide range of variables, such as *age*, *education*, (computer) *experience*, *computer-ownership* *(O/NO)* *gender* status *(M/F)*, *disability* *(D/ND)* status, with the psychometric variable, *computer-anxiety*; and finally examined in what manner computer-anxiety -assessed through a computer-anxiety score collected via Modified Computer Anxiety Scale (MCAS; Bhattacharjee, 2006), creates barriers to computer use and access for older adult users.

Thus the independent variables, *age-related-infirmity* *(W/WT)*, and *computer-anxiety* were tested for their degree

9

and nature of association with the outcome variable of the study *barriers-to-computer-use*. The barrier score (barrier_score alternatively scoreb) collected via Inherent Limitations of Systems and Web Design Scale (ILSWDS; Bhattacharjee, 2006), was utilized in assessing whether or not age induced infirmities, served as barrier factors in accessing and using computer technology for senior users (Howard, Murphy & Thomas, 1986). Similarly, the computer-anxiety score collected via Modified Computer Anxiety Scale (MCAS; Bhattacharjee, 2006) was used to determine whether computer-anxiety was truly a barrier factor for older adult user population's computer technology access.

More generally, the study:

1. Addressed directly or indirectly, the impact of all the above mentioned variables on the phenomenon of computer interaction for the older adult user groups.

2. Assessed the nature and direction of impact each variable has on their respective response/outcome variables.

More specifically the study:

1. Demonstrated the extent and nature of influence the variable *age* has on the variable *age-related-infirmity (W/WT)* within this specific population.

2. Demonstrated the extent and nature of influence of each of the variables *age*, *gender (M/F)*, *income*, *education*, *computer ownership (O/NO)*, (computer) *experience*, and *disability (D/ND)*, on the barrier variable *computer-anxiety*.

3. Assessed how the barrier variable *age-related-infirmity (W/WT)* correlates/associates with the response variable *barriers-to computer-use*.

10

4. Determined how the barrier variable *computer-anxiety* correlates/associates with the outcome variable *barriers-to-computer-use*.

The goal of the study was to understand the issue of computer interaction for the older adult user population, by specifically pointing out the psychosomatic and demographic factors which create impediments for senior users in their effort to access and use computer technology for information seeking and information manipulation purposes. The researcher, after analyzing users' feedback, identified the exact impact of each factor on barriers to computer technology access of senior users.

A prime objective of the study lay in decisively pointing out the areas which even distantly continue to create or alternatively ease barriers to computer interaction for senior citizens. The objectives of the study supported this primary goal. In addition the research:

1. Determined how users from the specified target group generally interact (frequency and intensity of such interaction) with computer technology, from within a web of socio-economic variables which the study presupposes defines their world as anxiety stricken users.

2. Determined how the underlying independent variable *age*, correlates/associates with the variable *age-related-infirmity (W/WT)*, also identified in the literature as a barrier factor.

3. Ascertained how each of the underlying independent variables, *age*, *gender (M/F)*, *income*, *education*, *computer ownership (O/NO)*, (computer) *experience*, *disability (D/ND)*, affect the immediate response variable *computer-anxiety* identified in the literature as a barrier factor.

11

Significance of the Problem

The research problem is significant because it deals with the issue of barriers in computer technology access of a user group, which despite its economic potential is considered to be information-technology-deprived. It is hoped that the execution of the study in the backdrop of a heavily wired university, with subjects who are educated, affluent and skilled, will play a crucial role in establishing or negating the credibility of factors known to determine the (varying) limits of older users' interaction with computer technology. The research gauges the magnitude and nature of impact of each of these factors on the computing behavior of older users. The goal was achieved through appropriate methods of data collection and analyses. The study results may be utilized to help unravel why the digital divide continues to afflict society's older population.

A major contribution of this research is its comprehensiveness; the research not only identified and explored two major barrier factors in computer technology access, for older users, and their actual association with the variable *"barriers-to-computer-use,"* but also analyzed the forces and factors which generate those barriers.

Research Questions

The research examined some underlying (socio economic and demographic) independent variables, along with two independent variables, *age-related-infirmity* (*W/WT*) and *computer-anxiety*, with a view to generally identifying the factors which directly or indirectly play a role in potentially raising or lowering the *barriers-to-computer-use* (the dependent variable of the study), from older users' perspectives. The research was driven by a set of research questions:

1. Does the variable *gender (M/F)* have a two-fold relationship with the variable *computer-anxiety*, for older adult users of the computer?

2. Is there a relationship between *computer-anxiety* on the one hand and each of the demographic variables, *income*, *education*, and (computer) *experience*, on the other?

3. Does the dichotomous variable *computer-ownership (O/NO)* have a two-fold relationship with the variable *computer-anxiety?*

4. Does the variable *disability (D/ND)* relate to *computer-anxiety* in a dichotomous fashion?

5. Does the demographic variable *age* affect the variable *computer-anxiety* in a direct fashion?

All the questions are related, in the sense all of them determined how the different socio-economic variables, such as *age*, *gender (M/F)*, *income*, *education*, *computer-ownership (O/NO)*, (computer) *experience*, and *disability (D/ND)*, correlate/associate with the psychological construct computer-anxiety, which in its turn plays a role, in (what literature confirms) affecting the nature of computer interaction patterns of older adult users in a negative fashion.

Based on research which have been conducted, the author came up with the following major hypotheses:

H1.The variable *age* has a two-fold relationship with the variable *age-related-infirmity (W/WT)*.

H2. There is a direct linear relationship between the variable *computer-anxiety* and the variable *barriers-to-computer-use*.

H3. The variable *age-related-infirmity* (*W/WT*) has a two-fold relationship with the dependent variable *barriers-to-computer-use*.

Definition of Terms

The following terms came up over and over again during the course of this study and are defined according to the author's intention to use them in the context of this research.

Aging- Aging signifies a continuous, universal and progressive process that brings with it such external changes as hair loss, graying hair, wrinkles and various other decrements, as well as not so perceptible internal changes, in the form of declining muscle strength, slowing immune system response, various disabilities, etc. ("Aging What is Aging," 2007).

Computer- The technology of the Internet embodies within itself computer technology, both being information technologies in essence. The Internet, if considered in terms of its protocols, embodies ways of exchanging information between two computers in a network or a collection of computers. Thus the computer and the Internet have developed to an extent whereby it becomes impossible to separate one from the other (Algharibi, 2005). Therefore, within the scope of this research, the term "computer use" is understood to encompass interaction with the Internet, as well.

Experience- Literature review reveals experience to be an important correlate of the variable *computer-anxiety*. The term, for the purpose of the present research mainly represents respondents' length of experience with computers, measured in years. The term was variously used as (computer or computing) experience; experience (with

14

computers or in computing); in the present research.
However, despite apparent dissimilarities between and among
them the terms signify one and the same thing.

Interface- The term "interface," in the context of this
study, signified the point where two systems meet and
communicate with each other and which incidentally is a
very pertinent feature for a wide spectrum of computer
/Internet technologies (Fisk, Wendy, Rogers, Charness,
Czaja & Sharit, 2004).

Older Adult- For the purpose of the present study, the
researcher used a definition which is adapted and
enunciated by DOEA, State of Florida. Expounding on the
broad meaning of the term, Bernice Neugarten of the
University of Chicago (as cited in Fulks, 2005) contends
that instead of classifying the elderly into a large group,
of "old," a subdivision should be made between the "old-
old" and the "young-old." Fulks (2005) thinks that it is
better to think of individuals as "young old" -ages between
55 and 74 and "old-old," individuals 75 and older. Fulks
asserts that this distinction has offered better
understanding of individuals from two important aspects -
peoples' functional abilities and their demographic
characteristics.

The Variables for the Study

The Dependent Variable

Barriers-to-Computer-Use: Researchers have shown that a
significant proportion of older adults encounter barriers
to computer use in the form of taking longer to learn to
use computers, making errors, taking longer to navigate,
etc. This can be attributed to the normal aging process,
which thwarts an older user's ability to successfully

15

interact with the standard graphical user interfaces. This sets apart the older users of computers, as a special user group with marked functionality difference in comparison to their younger counterparts. The inability on the part of the old to interact with the normal web interfaces can be found in the age-related cognitive, visual, auditory and musculoskeletal changes and disorders, which are known to be integral parts of the aging process. Cognitive changes among the old include reduction in processing speed and working memory and a decreased ability to ignore irrelevant and distracting information. Decline in cognitive abilities among the elderly may have some significant implications for technology access for the older users of computer systems. For example, declining cognitive faculties can prohibit older users from learning new skills like recalling complex operational procedures required for successful web navigation. Declining attentional capacity may make it difficult for older users to switch their attention between competing displays of information. They may also experience problems in attending to target information on an overcrowded website. Similarly, decline in vision may make reading a text on computer screens a difficult task for elderly people. Not only is it difficult for such users to read characters which are too small but also certain types of backgrounds can prevent them from reading the contents of web sites, even when text size has been maximized. Also, reduced musculo-skeletal capabilities prevent older users from successfully attending to input devices like keyboards and mouse. The study intended to find out the exact nature of the relationship between the dichotomous variable *age-related-infirmity* (*W/WT*) and the dependent variable *barriers-to-computer-use* (Zajicek, 2007;

16

Whitcomb, 2007; Czaja, 2007; Laux, McNally, Paciello &
Vanderheiden, 2007).

The psychometric variable *computer-anxiety* is posited
in the literature as a barrier factor as well, in access
and use of computer technology. The variable acts by
restraining users from exploiting the potentials of
computer technology to its fullest. Studies suggest that
people with high levels of computer-anxiety tend to avoid
computers and display a lower level of adjustment to
computer technology; also an inverse relation was
discovered between computer-anxiety and internet use. It
was found that people who tend to have higher levels of
computer-anxiety spend lesser amounts of time online. The
present study sought to find out the exact nature of
association between the variable *computer-anxiety* and the
variable *barriers-to-computer-use* (Smith & Caputi, 2007;
Barbiete & Weiss, 2004; Joiner, Brosnan, Duffield, Gavin &
Maras, 2007)

The Independent Variables

1. **Age -Related -Infirmity (W/WT)**: One possible reason for
older adults' aversion to computers can be linked to the
process of natural aging. This is because age is
accompanied by a host of changes in the areas of human
memory, motility measures, and motor mechanisms. Also,
decline in vision related and auditory capacities, bone
loss, and decrements in muscular and joint strength are
common phenomena of old age (Hanson, 2001; Zaphiris &
Kurniawan, 2001).

These factors are known to intervene with the
possibility of a smooth computer interaction for older
users, thereby creating barriers between the computer and
the user in the process. The present research intended to

17

explore the precise nature of association between this variable and the dependent variable, *barriers-to-computer use*. This is a dichotomous variable, represented at two levels (i) *with age-related infirmity* and (ii) *without age-related-infirmity (W/WT)*, postulated to have a two-fold relationship with the final outcome variable. This means that people who suffer from infirmities associated with old age have a greater likelihood of facing barriers in accessing and using computer technology than their counterparts who do not have such infirmities.

Underlying Independent Variable

Age: The variable *age* is postulated to have a direct linear relationship with the independent variable *age-related-infirmity (W/WT)*, thus it is assumed that the rate of occurrences of infirmities goes up with the increasing age of an individual.

2. **Computer-Anxiety**: It is estimated that a prime factor keeping older adults away from computers is computer-anxiety, a common emotional response to computers marked by explicit fear on the part of many adults. The present study intended to explore the exact nature of the relationship between this independent variable and the dependent variable, *barriers-to-computer-use*.

Underlying Independent Variables

Age: The present study focused on exploring the precise nature of the relationship between the underlying independent variable, *age*, and the independent variable *computer-anxiety*. The literature review confirmed that *age* is directly related to *computer-anxiety*.

18

Gender (M/F): The research explored the exact nature of the relationship between the underlying independent variable, *gender (M/F)* and the independent variable *computer-anxiety*. The literature review, however, reveals that males suffer from significantly less computer-anxiety than their female counterparts.

Income, Education, (Computer) *Experience, Computer Ownership (O/NO), Experience, Disability (D/ND):* These are important underlying independent variables found to be associated with computer-anxiety. The researcher tried to determine the exact nature of association each of these variables separately have with their outcome variable *computer-anxiety*. The literature review implied that an inverse relationship separately exists between the variable *computer--anxiety* and each of the variables *income, education,* (computer) *experience*. The variable *computer-ownership* a categorical dichotomous variable, with two levels *owners,* and *non-owners (O/NO),* is known to share a two-fold relationship with the variable *computer-anxiety;* thus a computer owner is likely to suffer from significantly lower levels of computer- anxiety, compared to his/her equivalent counterpart who does not own a computer.

The variable *disability,* a dichotomous variable with two levels, *disabled* and *not-disabled (D/ND)* is known to have a two-fold relationship with the outcome variable *computer-anxiety.* Thus it is assumed that a disabled person is prone to suffer from significantly higher levels of computer-anxiety than his/her equivalent counterpart without any disability.

Overview of Methodology

Measuring the Variables

The dependent variable of the study *barriers-to computer-use* was measured through respondents' self-reported perceptions about the degree of ease, inhibition or difficulty experienced in the use of standardized computer technology. Respondents' answers in this regard were recorded on a 5-point Likert-type scale, Inherent Limitations of Systems and Web Design Scale (ILSWDS; Bhattacharjee, 2006), with a lower score indicating lesser resistance or lesser amount of difficulty faced in interacting with features like background noise, blinking texts, scroll bars, mouse clicks etc., and a higher score signifying higher resistances faced by an individual in interacting with the stated features.

Similarly, respondents' *computer-anxiety* scores were recorded on a 5-item Likert-type scale, Modified Computer Anxiety Scale (MCAS; Bhattacharjee, 2006), with response categories ranging from "Strongly Agree," (5), to "Strongly Disagree," (1), with higher scores indicating higher levels of computer-anxiety, and lower scores signifying lower levels of computer-anxiety, faced by an individual user while in interaction with computers.

The other variables of the study were measured via concrete units or through "yes"/"no" type responses. *Age*, was measured in years. *Income* was measured in terms of USD (in 1000 United States dollars). *Education* was measured in terms of degrees earned. *Experience* (in computing) was measured in years. *Computer-ownership* (*O/NO*) was measured through "yes"/ "no" type response. Likewise, other dichotomous variables, such as *disability* (*D/ND*) and *age-*

20

related-infirmity (*W/WT*), were measured through "yes"/"no" type responses; only *gender* (*M/F*) was measured through dichotomous response categories of *male/female*.

Conceptual Framework: Overview of the Model

The researcher created a model (Fig. 1) to depict the barriers faced by the older adult user population (measured via barrier score representing the dependent variable, *barriers-to-computer-use*) in accessing computer technology, vis-a vis the key underlying independent variables and the independent variables (identified through the literature review) under the purview of the present study. The model (Fig. 1) presented here tried to closely simulate the real life forces, which are purportedly in operation, either directly or in an indirect fashion, to aid or constrain the prospect of an easier and less hindered computer interaction for older adult user groups. The intention of the researcher was to utilize this model (Fig. 1), with a view to unraveling, confirming and validating the conclusions reached in prior research about the direction of significant relationship/association the study's variables share with conterminous variables.

The demographic variables (*age*, *gender* (*M/F*), *income*, *education*, *computer-ownership* (*O/NO*) status, *experience* (with computers), and *disability* (*D/ND*) status) were included in the model to portray how each is related to the psychological construct computer-anxiety, described as a key barrier factor, which in turn was depicted as having a direct linear association with the dependent variable, b*arriers-to-computer-use*.

The underlying independent variable, a*ge*, was projected in the model and the direction of its causal relationship with the dichotomous independent variable *age-*

21

related-infirmity (*W/WT*) was underscored. The variable *age-related-infirmity*'s (*W/WT*) causal relationship with the final outcome variable of the study *barriers-to-computer-use* was also portrayed in the model.

Explanation of the Model

One of the underlying independent variables hypothesized to have a direct relationship with the phenomenon of computer-anxiety is *age*; this means that an older individual is more likely to suffer from computer-anxiety than his younger counterpart (ignoring all the other variables).

Underlying independent variables which were assumed to have a negative relationship with the variable *computer-anxiety* are *income*, *education*, and *experience* (with computing). Thus it is presumed that as a user's income, education, and/or computing experiences go up, he or she becomes less likely to suffer from computer-anxiety compared to someone who has lower levels of income, education and experience, ignoring all other variables (for each of the mentioned predictor variables).

The categorical-dichotomous independent variable *gender (M/F)* is known to share a two-fold relationship with the variable *computer-anxiety*. This means that a male computer user is less likely to suffer from higher levels of computer-anxiety than his equivalent female counterpart.

Similarly, the categorical-dichotomous variable *computer-ownership* (*O/NO*) is depicted as having a two-fold relationship with the independent variable *computer-anxiety*; which means that a person who owns a computer is less likely to suffer from computer-anxiety than his/her equivalent counterpart who does not own a computer.

The categorical-dichotomous variable *disability* (*D/ND*)
is depicted as having a two-fold relationship with the
variable *computer-anxiety*. Thus it is assumed that a person
with a disability is more likely to suffer from computer-
anxiety than his/her equivalent without a disability.

The independent variable *computer-anxiety*, in turn, is
presumed to have a direct relationship with the dependent
variable *barriers-to-computer-use*, which means that people
who suffer from computer-anxiety are more likely to face
barriers in accessing computer technology, ignoring all
other variables.

The left hand side of the model portrays *age* as having
a direct linear relationship with the variable, *age-
related-infirmity* (*W/WT*), a barrier factor. This may mean
that as the age of a user goes up, his/her probabilities of
suffering from infirmities increases.

The model portrays *age-related-infirmity* *(W/WT)*, a
categorical-dichotomous independent variable as having a
two-fold linear association with the test variable
barriers-to-computer-use, which means that a person
suffering from infirmities associated with old age is more
likely to face barriers in accessing computer technology
than his/her equivalent counterpart who does not suffer
from any infirmities.

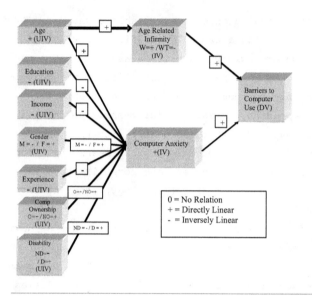

Figure 1. A model representing the assumed relationships among the variables of the study (Designed by Bonny Bhattacharjee)

```
How to interpret dichotomous relationships:
Example: Computer Ownership (O=-/NO=+) =A person who owns a computer is less likely to
suffer from computer anxiety (represented by a - sign signifying an inverse
relationship with the variable Computer Anxiety) compared to his /her counterpart who
does not own a computer (represented by a + sign signifying a direct linear
relationship with the variable Computer Anxiety).
```

Key:

```
    UIV- Underlying independent variable
    IV- Independent Variable
    DV- Dependent Variable
```

Limitations of the Study

The study was conducted at the main campus of Florida State University, a public institution of higher learning. The data for the study were collected from among the economically well-off permanent employees of Florida State University, both faculty and non-faculty. The elevated socio-economic status of FSU's employees is demonstrated by

facts which suggest that the average annual salary level of
a faculty member of FSU (for the year 2006-2007, providing
services on a 9 month contract basis), which ranges from
$98,000 to $76,000 depending on their designation, in a
descending order from Professor to Assistant Professor.
Statistics show that approximately 2,452 (USPS) University
Support Professional System and 1,978 (A &P) Administrative
& Professional employees, including 21 employees under
executive services, were earning an average salary of about
$ 54,153 annually for the current fiscal year (Florida
State Office of Institutional Research, 2007; Jianling,
personal communication, September 15, 2007).

Therefore, the results of the study were not
generalizable to the senior population, as such. This is a
major limitation of the study. Also, the author of the
study is aware of the fact that since the study qualifies
as an exploratory study, the model devised for the purpose
of the study has limited applicability.

The present chapter identified the purpose,
significance, and goals of the present research. It
proposed a set of research questions and hypotheses which
the study answered and tested, respectively. The chapter
also analyzed in detail the socio-economic and psychosomatic factors affecting older adults' computer
interaction behaviors, either directly or in an indirect
fashion. The next chapter reviews the literature the author
consulted in developing the study.

LITERATURE REVIEW

In the introduction, the author described older adults' relationship with information technologies - their lack of cultural conditioning vis a vis the latter and other psychological, physiological and demographic factors which mediate in important ways the specific user group's interaction with computer technology. In this chapter the researcher describes previous studies which helped her lay the foundation of an exact model comprising of factors, known to influence older adult users' interaction with computers.

Appendix A.1 is intended to help readers identify the instruments used during the course of the studies (cited in the literature review), along with a brief description of the measures. The appendix is by no means comprehensive as only standardized measures with names were discussed in the following appendix, along with the names of the researchers, exactly the way they have been presented in the study.

Similar Barrier Studies

A review of the literature reveals that similar studies analyzing the role of significant barrier factors (physiological and emotional) shaping older adults' computer usage have been conducted in the past.

Millward's (2003) study, for which data were collected for qualitative analyses by using a questionnaire from 58 participants (24 males and 34 females, in the age range 71 -80), affirmed that some important factors prevent older adult users from using the Internet. The factors as stated by Millward (2003): are cost of connection, the high price of a computer, lack of knowledge about computer technology, and lack of motivation to use computer technology.

Richardson, Zorn, and Weaver (2005), in a study executed to assess the barriers, benefits, negative consequences, and gender differences in older New Zealander's use of computers, identified seven major categories of barriers that older adults experience. They are 1) lack of positive attitudes towards computers, 2) declining faculties, 3) financial costs, 4) unfamiliarity with the technology, 5) age-unfriendly instructions, 6) lack of perceived relevance /motivation, and 7) lack of social support. The research was driven by two research questions: the first one, and the most important one from the perspective of this study, inquired about the barriers, benefits and negative consequences associated with learning and using computers, and the second one probed the major differences between elderly males' and elderly females' perception about the major barriers, benefits and negative consequences pertaining to learning and using computers.

The study's findings revealed that learning how to use computers is an emotional experience for older adults, particularly for older adult women. Both men and women reported that failing eyesight and arthritic or shaky hands inhibited their ability to read computer screen displays, and prevented them from controlling the mouse and finding information on the screen. Participants also reported having problems with computer jargon and typing skills; computer jargon was deemed as a foreign language, or something designed for specific professionals like engineers. On the financial side, respondents reported that the price of computers was an important barrier to their use of computers. Also, age unfriendly instructions were

27

reported as a factor inhibiting their interaction with computer technology. The respondents also cited lack of relevance and motivation as potential barriers to computer interaction. Lack of perceived need to use computers thus figured as a major stumbling block to older people's learning about how to use computers. Also, the absence of long-term social support from relatives and significant others in inducing older adults into sustained computer usage was cited as a significant barrier to computer use by the respondents. This is important because the issue of social support was cited by older adults as an important issue that helped them overcome the barriers they faced in their endeavor to learn and use computers. A perceptible limitation of the study is its lack of generalizability, since Senior Net, where the participants for the study were drawn from, is a socio-economically privileged group of mainly white, educated senior adults.

Gietzelt (2001) conducted a study in Australia to determine the phenomena of older adults' fear of and motivations behind Internet use. The final participants of the study were part of a convenience sample drawn, based on criteria like age (55 years or older), computer ownership *(O/NO)* and local residency status.

A questionnaire was generated for the purpose of the study from an examination of the relevant literature. The questionnaire consisted of three sections. The first section sought information concerning respondents' computer use and their self perception about their skills in computing. The second section gathered data about respondents' Internet use, and the third section gathered demographic data about the respondents. Questions in the questionnaire were both open and close-ended.

The participants consisted of 13 females and 20 males between the ages of 55 and 79 years. Almost half of the respondents (45%) had not completed high school, and only 6 respondents (15%) had completed university. Thirty percent of the respondents were employed and about 60% were engaged in unpaid or voluntary labor. Twenty-nine (88%) of the respondents had a computer at home, and over 90% of those who had a computer at home accessed that home computer. Thirteen percent used computers in their local library, six percent used computers at a local computer club or at their work place and about three percent accessed computers from colleges and universities.

The barriers to Internet use as cited by the participants arose out of personal limitations like vision-related problems for 16% of the participants. Also, 28% of the respondents cited technological barriers which included computer breakdowns and malfunctioning, inability to download and inability to access required sites.

Introduction to the variables affecting the Barrier

The present study, much like the above studies, tried to discern the effect of variables which the literature suggests create barriers to computer technology access for older adult users. Such variables identified for this research are: 1.*Age-related-infirmity (W/WT)* 2.*Computer-anxiety.*

1.*Age-related-infirmity (W/WT)*: Identified in the literature as a major barrier factor to access, for older users of computer technology, was examined closely in this study, along with its predictor variable (underscored in this study as underlying independent variable), *age*. The variable was tested for the precise nature of its relationship with the ultimate response variable of the

29

study *barriers-to-computer-use*.

Age-related-infirmity: Predictor Variable

Age: The reason why *age* was chosen as a predictor variable for *age-related-infirmity* (*W/WT*) is because the literature review confirmed that the rate of occurrences of human impairments (which are known to hinder older users of computers from effectively accessing the technology), increases with age. Generally, these impairments include cognitive and musculoskeletal disorders, vision and auditory impairments, etc. These otherwise abstract barrier factors which are known to plague the physically challenged computer-users, among the old, assume identifiable forms, when say a vision-impaired individual due to his/her inherent inability to read computer text is compelled to reject a standard computer and is forced to demand a computer with special assistance tools like larger screen, and a speech output system that reads the on-screen text; or when a user with a musculoskeletal impairment is forced to demand a special keyboard with enlarged keys so as to avoid hitting more than a single key at a time("Access to Computer," 2006, O Brian, 2007).

How does the variable *age-related-infirmity* work as a barrier factor?

Problems associated with the physiology of old age have been identified by researchers as a factor affecting use of computers among the older users of technology. The International Federation of Library Associations and Institutions conducted a study to demonstrate that psycho-physiological variables like attitudes and faltering

30

physiological systems in older adults affect their
interaction with computers ("Older People and the
Internet,"1997). The study, a field study, involved older
adult respondents (50 years and above), who were asked to
nominate statements which they thought well reflected the
role computers play in their lives. Sixty-seven percent of
the respondents reported that they have negative attitudes
towards computers, 42% thought that they would never need
to use computers as they were not relevant to their lives,
and 25% thought they would use a computer only if they
really had to. In addition, older adults reported a host of
physiological barriers which kept them from using computer
technologies to the fullest extent. About 67% reported
having problems with pointing, scrolling, and clicking of
the mouse. While some of the older adults thought that
their capacity to manipulate the mouse would improve with
practice, others who were suffering from arthritis or
tremors and were incapable of fine movements reported that
it would not. Also, about 30% of the respondents complained
about their inability to read a computer screen ("Older
People and the Internet," 1997).

Williamson, Bow, and Wale (1997) examined the human-
factor-related issues associated with computer interfaces
as hindrances to older adults' use of computers, in the
context of a study conducted to discern how access to
Internet technology can be improved for older adult users.
The research was conducted using both survey and
observation methods and was carried out in the venues
offered by three libraries at Brighton, Box Hill, and
Hamilton, in Australia.

It was found that barriers to new technologies can
come in the form of negative feelings and attitudes toward

31

new technologies that make people less likely to use them.
It was revealed that for those over the age of 50 years the
technology of computers did not evoke particularly positive
feelings. Only about one-fifth of the older adults studied
expressed some positive feelings towards using a computer.
Most of the participants in the second part of the study
(about 90% of them) had never used the Internet before the
observation session, and 85% said they would not use it
again. The most frequent problems that older adults had
with Internet use were difficulties in searching the web,
which arose because of a seeming lack of navigation skills.
The participants had some major problems with using the
mouse, for pointing, clicking and scrolling. While
approximately one-fifth of the sample (21%) had extensive
problems with using the mouse, even more (about 24%) had
problems with scrolling. Thirty percent of the participants
reported that they had problems reading the screen due to
small print size or the color. Thirty percent also
expressed frustrations about the general lack of
instructions on using the Internet, while 20% of the
participants were extremely frustrated by the time delays
in getting information from the Internet.

The other barrier factor

2. *Computer-anxiety*: Also identified as a barrier to
access, the variable was examined closely. To that extent,
the present study examined the most relevant factors which
are known to cause computer-anxiety in older users, such
as, *age*, *income*, *education*, (computer) *experience*, the
dichotomous variables *gender (M/F)*, *computer-ownership
(O/NO)*, and *disability (D/ND)*. The nature and extent of
association between the independent variable *computer-
anxiety*, and the outcome variable of the study *barriers-to-*

32

computer-use, was also evaluated in turn.

A common psychosomatic phenomenon which affects older adults' interaction with computers is computer-anxiety. Computer-anxiety, as defined by Howard, Murphy and Thomas (1986), is the "fear of impending interaction with a computer that is disproportionate to the actual threat presented by the computer". Orr (2007) is of the opinion that computer-anxiety is a specific anxiety type that occurs under specific kinds of situations. Fajou (1997) contends that those who are computer-anxious experience negative emotions like frustration, fear of the unknown, fear of possible failure, embarrassment, disappointment, etc.

Rosen and Weil (1987) have identified three levels of computer-anxiety. The first is what they call an anxious "technophobe," a person who exhibits some classic symptoms of anxiety reaction, like sweaty palms, headaches, etc. The second type is a "cognitive technophobe," a person who on the surface is quite relaxed, but is internally suffering from negative perceptions about his/her actual ability to use technology. The third type is an "uncomfortable user," whom the authors dub as a slightly anxious user. Studies reveal that older adults are known to exhibit the unique symptoms of technophobes.

Lantis & Sulewski (1994) aver that older adult users of computer technology show signs of instinctive fear towards technology; this fear/anxiety varies from minor stress in some to full-fledged cyber-phobia or fear of computers in others.

Norris (2001) blames the differences in computer usage to a generational gap, resulting in older adults' slow adaptation to the technology of Internet and general lack

of experience. It has been found that humiliation in
failing to use technology is a major fear of older people
(Millward, 2003).

Other studies confirm the presence of a "fear factor"
behind abysmally low Internet usage rates among older
adults:

> In examining this statistic more closely, we discover
> that only 11% of older adults use the Internet. Why is
> the percentage of users so low? The reason is simple.
> Like everything else in life, people tend to fear what
> they do not understand. It is my hypothesis that if
> older adults are introduced to the relevance,
> usefulness and/or enjoyment of the Internet and if
> they have the concepts broken down into useable
> pieces, they will be more inclined to use it ("Older
> Adults and the Internet," 2004, p.1).

The existing literature, identified anxiety as a
barrier which if present in excess or in lower amounts
yield lower levels user performances (Desai & Richards,
1998; Mikulincer et al.,1990; Berntsen, 2005).

How does the variable *computer-anxiety* work as a barrier factor?

Research has been conducted to determine how computer-
anxiety thwarts the prospects of computer use and access
from the perspective of users.

Anthony, Clarke and Anderson (2000) undertook research
examining the levels of technophobia in a sample of 176
students in a university in South Africa. The primary aim
of the study was to determine whether computer-anxiety is
correlated with each of the five dimensions of personality
(neuroticism, extroversion, openness, agreeableness,

conscientiousness). The sample was a mix of men and women and was fairly representative of the university's student population. The study was conducted using Rosen and Weil's Measuring Technophobia Instruments (MTI;1992), which was slightly modified to suit South African culture; and the NEO-Five Factor Inventory {NEO-FFI (Form S)}, a shortened version of the NEO Personality Inventory (NEO-PI-R; Costa & McCrae,1985).The instruments were found to be reliable. Subjects were randomly chosen from psychology, computer science and end-user computing courses.

The data collected for the study indicated that computer-anxiety is related to neuroticism, a phenomenon associated with one's susceptibility to the level of distress. It was surmised that people with high neuroticism tend to react with higher levels of anxiety and stress when exposed to a computing environment. A neurotic individual responds to stress by adopting an avoidant coping approach and consequently exhibits lower levels of adjustment to computer technology.

Joiner et al. (2007), conducted a study with an aim to investigate the relationship between Internet-anxiety and Internet use. The participants were 446 students, out of which 319 were females and 127 were males. The students were chosen from two universities in the United Kingdom and one university in Australia. Two measures were developed to assess students' use of the Internet. The first was a Likert-type measure to determine students' use of the Internet generally, the seven items of the measure consisted of e-mail, chat, newsgroups, online games, sex sites, shopping and music sites etc. The second measure aimed at determining how often students used the Internet for university coursework. A scale was developed to measure

35

computer-anxiety levels of the students. The data revealed that Internet-anxiety was negatively related to general Internet use and Internet- anxiety was negatively related to hours per week of Internet usage.

Mcilroy, Sadler, and Boojawon (2007) undertook a study to ascertain if students with high anxiety, low positive cognition, and low self-efficacy were less likely to exploit the range of facilities provided for them by the university. The sample of undergraduate students from a university in Liverpool was comprised of 363 females and 261 males. The mean age of the sample was 24.51 years, and they came from disciplines like economics, consumer studies, counseling, business, language, etc. Three measures were used for this study: the Computer Anxiety Rating Scale (CARS; Rosen & Weil, 1992), a 20 -item Likert type scale; and the Computer Thoughts Survey (CTS; Rosen & Weil, 1992), also a 20-item Likert-type scale in which responses are scored on statements like 1-"not at all," to 5="very often," and a computer self efficacy scale originally used by Murphy, Coover, and Owen, in 1989. The reliability coefficients of the scales were assessed as being robust. Students were asked whether they completed a computer course, whether their initial experience with computers was positive or negative and whether they used a computer in the home environment, etc. Students were also asked to rate on a 5-point Likert-type scale the extent to which they assessed the university computer facilities which were www, e-mail, electronic journals and several Microsoft facilities, like Word, Excel, and PowerPoint. About 20% of the students were identified as moderate to highly computer phobic as evidenced by the CARS (1992) and the CTS (1992) cut-off points. Data analysis revealed that

36

computer-anxiety as a variable is negatively correlated to the use of university facilities; thus it was concluded that students with computer-anxiety tend not to exploit university offered computer facilities to their fullest potentials. It was thus assumed that the computer phobes experience some inhibition in computer use and performance.

A host of factors influence *computer-anxiety* among older users of computer technology; however, for the purpose of the present study we shall focus on demographic variables like users' *age*, *experience* (with computing), *education*, *income*, *gender* (*M/F*) status, *computer-ownership* (*O/NO*) status, and *disability* (*D/ND*) status, in trying to discern how each variable individually relates to the variable *computer-anxiety*.

Computer-anxiety: Predictor Variables

Age: Anderson (2005) indicated that senior citizens use Internet less frequently than younger users, in the United Kingdom.

A study conducted by Hintze and Lehnus (2004) discovered an inverse relationship between age and Internet use. They report that while in the year 1997, 67% of 16 to 19-year-old males in the study had accessed the Internet, only 61% percent of males in the age bracket of 20-24 accessed the same technology – an authentication of the fact that the level of technology usage is less among the older people when compared to their younger counterparts.

Another study found that only 29% of Americans aged 65 years and older use computers on an occasional basis, and only about 2 in 10 off-line seniors entertain the thought of going on-line at all. For the rest of the seniors,

computer/Internet technology is pretty much off-limits
("Older Americans and the Internet," 2004).

In contrast to older adults the younger adults, like
children, and teenagers, are more likely to use computers.
Computer usage is also high among people in their prime
workforce years - from 20s through 50s ("A Nation Online:
How Americans are Expanding their Use of the Internet,"
2002).

Kelley and Charness (1995) contend that missing out on
an environmental advantage provided by the culture of
technology, a phenomenon that their younger counterparts
enjoy, has hit the older adult population hard, thereby
making adjustment to technology a difficult task for them.

This might also explain why older adults' failed to
become a comprehensive part of the computer culture. As
Rotstein (1999) asserts with respect to a specific user:

> He's a part of a generation that missed out on
> computers in the workplace, but sees everyone from
> friends to grandchildren becoming proficient with them
> now, and doesn't want to feel isolated because of
> computer illiteracy (p.1).

It is obvious that fear, a general negative attitude
and lack of experience will have an impact on older adults'
levels of computer-anxiety. Research on age in relation to
computer-anxiety, some of which are cited in the present
study, has proven to be inconclusive, albeit a large
proportion of the studies reveal a higher degree of
computer anxiety in older learners.

Laguna and Babcock (1997) conducted a study with the
intention of examining the construct of computer-anxiety in
young and older adults. The subjects of the study were 20

38

young adults, in the age bracket of 18-27 years, and 20 older adults, in the age range of 55 to 82 years. There were 10 men and 10 women in each group. The participants were made to do a computer based task in the aftermath of which their computer-anxiety scores were collected using a Computer Anxiety Index (CAIN; Montag, Simonson, & Maurer, 1984). The authors concluded that older adults suffered from significantly higher levels of computer-anxiety compared to their younger counterparts.

Ellis and Allaire (1999) surveyed 330 older adults (78% female in the age range of 60 to 97 years with an average age of 78 years), to assess the effects of variables such as *age*, *education*, (computer) *experience* and *computer-anxiety* on computer interest in older adults. Data on respondents' computer-anxiety level were garnered via a 10-point Likert-type scale known as the Raub scale (Raub; 1982). Similarly the respondents' scores on computer interest and computer knowledge were collected via separate 5-point Likert-type scales. The authors discovered that computer-anxiety is directly related to age. Dyck and Smither's (1994) study, cited above, however, indicated that older adults were less computer-anxious, and had more positive attitudes toward computers.

Butchko (2000) studied a group of volunteer participants (17.9% males and 82.1% females whose ages ranged from 19 -67 years with a mean age of 35 years), to determine whether *age* as a variable predicts anxiety toward computers and computer technology. The participants for Butchko's (2000) study were tested for their computer experience. Participants were asked to rate each item on a 5-point Likert scale from 1 (Never) to 5 (Daily). A

component of the questionnaire was the 20-item Computer
Anxiety Scale (CAS; Marcoulides, 1989). Subjects used a 5-
point Likert format to reflect their anxiety ranging from 1
(Not at all) to 5 (Very much). The results revealed that
there is no significant relationship between the variables
age and *computer-anxiety*.

Several researchers are of the opinion that technology
has some degree of acceptance among a cross-section of
older adults. Several studies reveal that older adults not
only evince a high degree of interest in computers but also
have the potential to learn how to use them (Echt, Morrell,
& Park, 1998; Kelley et al. 1999; and Morrell, Park,
Mayhorn & Echt, 1996).In the same vein, Hargrove and
Stempel (2002) concluded that at least a sub-section of the
older adult population (those below the age of 65) are
extremely Internet-savvy.

Gender(M/F): The variable *gender* *(M/F)* also plays a role in
computer technology use. A study by Donald Teel (2004)
states that 37% of senior men go online as compared to only
14% of senior women. Researchers have identified some
concrete causes behind female users' apparent apathy/
dislike towards computers. A well- documented one in this
regard centers around the issue of differential access to
computers.

Speaking of gender imbalance in general, in matters
pertaining to computer ownership, and usage, Flethcher-
Flinn & Suddendorf (1996) contend that a skewed scenario
favoring the males can be found throughout the academic
life of average student users, from elementary school to
high school and right into college.

40

Shashaani (1994) affirmed that among secondary school students, more male than female students report having a home computer and the same gender-related difference is reported by students at the university level (Shashaani, 1997). Jenson (1999) states that relatively less computer experience for the girls, at home and at school, also work to exacerbate their disadvantage with respect to computers.

Koch (1995) avers that in the classroom as well, male students have a greater tendency to monopolize available computer resources during free time and females will only use them when instructed.

The low level of computer exposure among female students likely results in a narrower range of computer experience among this gender group, while male students are known to have a wider range of experiences with computers (Shashaani, 1994; Comber et al., 1997).

Also, owing to a relatively narrow range of experience with computers, female students report lower confidence levels in matters pertaining to computer usage and subsequently lower levels of interest in computers (Shashaani 1994; Sashaaani 1997; Volman 1997). Lack of access and experience, in turn, trigger among the females a negative attitude towards computers, and they end up perceiving them as a gender-tinged technology belonging to the male spheres of mathematics, science and electronics (Inkpen, et al., 1994).

Studies show that differences in boys and girls with respect to computer attitudes are fairly crystallized at the age of three, and boys aged 3-6 already have a gender stereotyped view of users (Davies et al. 2005).

It was presumed that following this trend of differential gender-based attitudes and experiences with

41

respect to computers, some sort of difference would be found in the studies examined about how older users, of both genders, variously view computer technology.

Dyck and Smither (1994) in a study conducted on two groups of computer users - one group of older users (55 years of age and older) and the other group of younger users (30 years and younger) - however, found no gender difference in computer-anxiety, although the relationship between computer experience and computer preference were found to be lower among the females than the males. Morrow, Prell, and McElroy (1986) and Raub (1981) did find a gender difference in the level of perceived computer-anxiety, with women exhibiting higher levels of computer-anxiety.

Richardson, Zorn, and Weaver (2005), in a study conducted on older users of computer technology, noticed some differences in older users' perceptions of technology, on the basis of their gender. Women were found to express greater amount of fear about both learning and using computers and expressed lack of confidence regarding the technology more often than their male counterparts. The male participants of the study, while not as anxious, suffered from other emotional or attitudinal barriers like "unknown void" and "frustration" with respect to the idea of computer use.

Ogozalek (1994) conducted a study of older participants, both males and females (ages in the range of 65-75 years), to determine whether gender differences exist regarding how men and women view computers. Information was presented to participants via leaflets and computer-based interfaces (text-based and multimedia interfaces) with a view to determining which medium communicated ideas more effectively. The study also gathered data about respondents' performance and attitude towards computers via surveys. The results of the study seem to suggest that women possessed more negative attitudes toward computers and were more apprehensive of computer malfunctioning, fearing break-downs and related inconvenience, etc., than their male counterparts. Women also expressed a preference for more user-friendly multimedia interfaces than did the males. Men, on the other hand, were found to be more obsessively taken with the "machine-ness" of the gadget, and rather preferred to communicate with a computer than with a human being.

McIlroy et al. (2001) conducted a study to determine gender differences on a university population with regard to two measures: the Computer Anxiety Rating Scale (CARS; Rosen & Weil, 1992) and the Computer Thoughts Survey (CTS; Rosen & Weil, 1992). The measures of the scales reflect anxious attitudes (CARS, 1992), and negative/positive cognitions to computing (CTS, 1992). The sample for the study was comprised of 193 first year undergraduate social science students (157 females and 36 males) mostly in psychology. The average age of the participants was 22 years. The two gender groupings were comparable in age and educational background and were of the same ethnic origin. The research instruments were in the form of a booklet. The booklets requested some biographical information and questions relating to background experiences in computing, like the respondents' familiarity with computers, frequency of access to computing facilities outside the university, whether initial experiences with computers was positive or negative etc. Also, questions were asked about grades in computing at General Certificate of Secondary Education (GCSE) and Irish Junior Certificate level (the Irish

43

equivalent of GCSE). There were no significant differences in positive computing cognitions (reflected by CTS, 1992) for gender. In the CARS (1992), no significant differences in anxiety attitudes were revealed for the variable gender, or for regularity of access to computing facilities outside the university. However, positive attitudes were evident in those who were male and who had access to computing facilities outside the university. The CARS (1992) also revealed that there were significant differences in gender in terms of first computing experience and GCSE/Irish computing attainment (for anxiety attitudes). Respondents who had low anxiety on this measure were male, had a positive first experience in computing and had a GCSE/Irish or Irish Junior Certificate pass in computing. The CTS (1992) revealed that males who had regular access to computing facilities had more positive computing cognitions.

Brosnan (1999) conducted a study to identify the factors which predicted word processor usage over a 13-week semester among 147 psychology freshmen. There were 41 males and 144 females, ages ranged from 18 to 45 years, with a mean age 21.55 years. Students were asked to complete a battery of questionnaires, containing the Computer Anxiety Rating Scale (CARS; Heinssen, Glass & Knight, 1987). A computer self-efficacy test (Hill, Smith & Mann, 1987) was also administered. Computer attitudes were assessed using a 5-point Likert type questionnaire (Todman & Dick, 1993). Estimates of current word-processing usages and intended word-processing over the 13-week semester were obtained on a 7-point scale. Information about demographics such as sex, age, age of first computer interaction, non-word processing software, and programming experience were

44

requested together with whether the subject owned a computer or not. At the end of a 13-week semester subjects were asked to report how often they had used the computer during the semester, on the scale described already. Within the present sample, no sex differences in computer-anxiety were identified. The only significant gender differences were in the age of initial (computer) experience and the perception of computers as "fun." Males' initial (computer) experience typically occurred three years before females,' and males reported perceiving computers as being more fun than females did.

Durndell and Haag (2002) performed a study to determine the relationship between computer-anxiety, and computer self-efficacy, and attitudes toward the Internet and Internet experience among men and women, with an average age of 21.5 years. The sample consisted of 150 participants, 76 of whom were male and 74 of whom were female. The instruments for the study consisted of Computer Anxiety Rating Scale (CARS; Heinssen, Glass & Knight, 1987) to assess an individual's level of computer-anxiety. The Internet Attitude Scale (IAS), a modified version of Computer Attitude Scale (CAS; Nickell & Pinto, 1986), was used to determine the participants' attitude towards the Internet for the purpose of the study. The Computer Self Efficacy Scale (CSE; Torkzadeh & Koufteros, 1994) was used as an instrument for the study, as well, with some modification. A significant gender variation was found on all the measures. An average female reported a smaller time of use of the Internet, less positive attitudes towards the Internet, greater computer-anxiety and lower computer self efficacy vis a vis computers than males.

45

Sam, Othman, and Nordin (2005) conducted a study on 81 female and 67 male undergraduates to assess the undergraduates' computer-anxiety, computer self-efficacy, and attitudes towards the Internet. The subjects for this study were 148 undergraduates (at Universiti Malaysia Sarawak Unimas). The mean age of the subjects was 23.8 years, with the majority of the subjects being in the 19-23 years age bracket. The research instruments for the study included a questionnaire which was used to collect data for the study. The questionnaire collected demographic characteristics of the respondents such as age, race, gender and faculty etc. It also required of the subjects to report how much time in a week they used the Internet and the uses which the Internet was used for. The questionnaire also contained the Computer Anxiety Rating Scale (CARS; Heinssen, Glass & Knight, 1987), and the Computer Self Efficacy Scale (CSE; Torkzadeh & Koufteros, 1994; Murphy, Coover, & Owen, 1989). It was revealed that on average the undergraduates spent 9.2 hours in a week; 23 (15.5%) of the undergraduates reported using the Internet on average 10 hours in a week while 11 undergraduates (7.4%) used the Internet for 14 hours in a week. There were no differences in the undergraduates' usage pattern with the Internet based on gender. There were also no differences in the undergraduates' Internet usage levels, as measured by the time they spent on using the Internet, based on gender. The responses to the CARS (1987) revealed that the undergraduates have moderate computer-anxiousness. There were, however, no significant differences in computer-anxiety levels, attitude toward the Internet, and computer-self-efficacy based on gender, among the respondents.

46

An analysis of the study results cited above do
suggest that a majority of older women users find computers
to be a remote technology, something that is unpredictable
and about which they have considerable fear, anxiety and
apprehension, in contrast to their male counterparts.

Income: A study entitled "Falling through the Net II:
New data on digital divide" (2007) affirms that income
greatly affects technology penetration level. The report
describes the technological disparity among certain cross-
sections of the population in the following manner:

> Although all income groups are now more likely to own
> a computer, the penetration levels for those at higher
> incomes have grown more significantly. As a result,
> the gap in computer ownership levels between higher-
> income households and lower-income households have
> expanded in the last three years. For example, the
> difference in PC-ownership levels between households
> earning $10,000-$14,000 and those earning $50,000-$
> 74,999 was 47.7 percentage points in 1997, up from
> 38.2 percentage points in 1994(p.3).

The above passage more than emphatically points out how
income levels affect individual households' capacity to
keep up with the ongoing process of technological
adaptation. It also points towards the positive impact of
income on the issue of computer-ownership and access, this
is supported by the findings of a study entitled "Falling
Through the Net: Toward Digital Inclusion" (2000) which
describes the connection between income and the issue of
ownership and access in the following manner:

> Although computers and Internet access are coming down
> in price, they are still sufficiently expensive that
> household income remains an important factor in home

internet access ("Falling Through the Net: Toward Digital Inclusion," 2000).

Indeed a staggering eighty-seven percent of older adults living in households with income levels of $75,000 or more tend to have a computer, compared to about 28% of the adults living in households with an income of $25,000 or less ("Home Computers an Internet Use in the United States: August 2000," 2001).

The correlation between income and Internet use becomes clear from a study that claims that individuals over the age of 50 years are thrice as likely to be Internet users if they are participating in the labor force than if they are not ("Falling through the Net: Toward Digital Inclusion," 2000). Although no first hand data suggesting a clear-cut relationship between income and computer-anxiety could be found, it is assumed that higher income, by guaranteeing greater access to computers and thus greater experience with the same, helps to instill in relatively affluent users a greater amount of computer knowledge and competence, thereby helping to lower computer-anxiety levels among them.

A study by Bozionelos (2004) conducted for determining the relationship between the variables *income* and *computer-anxiety* suggests the same conclusion. The study was performed on a sample of 267 native speakers of English, both males and females (76%). About 52.5% of the participants were in the first year of study, 21.9% were in their second year of study, and 25.6% were in their third year of study.

Information about the background of the respondents were gathered using a simple item which requested the

48

respondents to indicate the socio-economic level of
their family on a 5-point scale. The respondents'
scores on computer-anxiety were collected on a 5-point
CARS (Computer Anxiety Rating Scale; Rosen & Weil,
1992). In another 10-item scale respondents were asked
to indicate their frequency of computer use, which
included software, hardware and networking products.
Respondents' scores on computer access were collected using
a 5-point scale.

The findings of the study suggested that socio-
economic status and the magnitude of computer use were
directly related via their relationships with (computers)
experience and computer-anxiety. The study underlined the
fact that people with higher socio-economic statuses were
more prone to accessing and using computers; hence were
more experienced with computers; and thus suffered from
less from computer-anxiety.

Education: Most of the "wired" seniors have a modest to
high level of education. In the year 2000, 36% of all
seniors using the Internet had attended college, and about
25% of Internet-savvy older adults had a high school
education (Older Americans and the Internet, 2004). Another
report ("Home Computers and Internet Use in the United
States: August 2000," 2001) concludes that the most highly
educated adults are the ones most likely to own computers.

By measuring computer-ownership, in terms of the
ability of older adults to access computers from their
homes, researchers found that 78% of the adults with a
bachelor's degree and beyond could access computers from
home, compared to only 46% of the adults with only a high
school diploma. In 2004, 62% of the wired seniors claimed
to have at least some college education; also 33% of the

49

Net-savvy older adults had attended school (Older Americans and the Internet, 2004).

The literature suggests a negative or inverse linear relationship between the variables *education* and *computer-anxiety*. Ellis and Allaire (1999) suggest, at the conclusion of their study, that higher levels of education were related to higher levels of computer-knowledge and computer-interest and thus lower levels of computer-anxiety. The data leading to this conclusion were collected from the responses of 330 participants; with an average age of 78 years. The participants responded to 5-point Likert-scale type questionnaires, which tested the level of their computer-knowledge and computer-interest. The limitations of the study (conducted on a handpicked sample from 16 senior-citizen apartment buildings in the Detroit Metropolitan area) notwithstanding, the authors' opinion that higher levels of education are related to lower levels of computer-anxiety among computer users, seems valid, especially in light of similar results from other studies, some of which are stated here.

Ray and Minch (1990) also assert that computer-anxiety seems to be less prevalent among users who are accomplished students (as indicated by their grade point average), and pay attention to news about computers, and rely on books to gather knowledge about them. The authors found that computer-anxiety is a good indicator of one's overall grade in courses pertaining to computers and to grades in academics, as such, concluding that higher levels of education are related to lower levels of computer-alienation (a construct which the authors used for the study to predict user reactions to computers – in terms of grades earned in a computer class, satisfaction with past

computer experiences, etc.) and hence lower levels of
computer-anxiety.

Yang, Mohamed and Beyerbach's (1999) study carried out
on a sample of 245 educators, whose ages ranged from under
29 years to over 50 years, was aimed at determining the
relationship between the variables *computer-anxiety* and
education; it established that a user's educational level
has an impact on the degree of computer-anxiety experienced
by him/her. The authors are of the opinion that educated
users were more confident in using computers (than users
with less education), and hence suffered less from
computer-anxiety.

It is assumed that higher levels of education, by
helping individuals maintain their intellectual and
cognitive abilities well into old age, aid better
interaction with computers, a technology that is known to
place considerable demand on individuals' working memory.

For example, due to advanced age, older people are
likely to experience more problems with performing mental
computations, because the combined storage and processing
requirements of such tasks tend to exceed the capacities of
their working memory. Along the same lines, working memory
limitations are known to interfere with older adults'
abilities to perform computer-based tasks. Poor memory
structure, it is suggested, hinders older people's
abilities to grapple with such computer-based tasks as
keeping track of complex databases or file records.

Researchers are of the opinion that decrements in
working memory due to aging, and subsequent decline in
reasoning abilities interfere with computer-based tasks
which require integration of information. On one occasion
the older participants (from among 65 subjects with ages

ranging from 20 to 75 years) derived fewer correct solutions for inventory management tasks, which required them to access the correct data files and integrate numeric information across files. Working memory limitations made it difficult for older adults to remember which information is contained in which file and interfered with their ability to maintain the information and perform the calculations necessary for problem solution (Sharit & Czaja, 1994; Charness, 1985; Salthouse, 1990).

Education, by aiding better cognitive performances in computer interaction, helps educated older users to interact more frequently and intensively with computers. Hence they end up suffering less from computer-anxiety.

The conclusion seems especially true in light of the fact that it is the less educated in society who tend to suffer the most from the adverse impact of the digital divide (Hockey et al., 1989; Dutta, 1992).

Computer-Ownership (O/NO): Researchers put forward the access issue as standing between older adults and "digital inclusion" ("Digital Inclusion in Northern Ireland," 2005). For example, Hargittai (2003) talks about "autonomy of use," as an important factor affecting Internet inequality. Under autonomy of use he lists factors like location of access and freedom to use the medium of the Internet for activities one prefers as major factors influencing digital inequality at the level of the individual.

In his article, Hargittai (2003) states:

> People who have access to top quality computers
> with good and reliable Internet connections at
> home or at work are much more likely to exhibit
> high levels of sophistication than those without
> access to such technical resources. Better

hardware, better software and faster connection
are the infrastructural basis of having access to
all that the Web has to offer. (p.11)

In the above passage the author talks about the
significance of access/ownership in lending the users of
the Internet the much needed knowledge to exploit its
potentials.

The nature of association between computer-ownership
(*O/NO*) and computer-competence was borne out by a study
conducted by McInerney, McInerney, and Sinclair (1990);
although the main aim of the study was to analyze the
effects of increased (computer) experience on computer-
anxiety levels of teacher education students, some
secondary data generated by the study also supported the
fact that PC ownership leads to increased computer
competence. The study was conducted on 101 participants out
of whom 21 were males and 80 females (mean age 21 years),
at a regional university in Australia. Sixty-five of these
students referred to them as beginners with regard to
computers, while 36 classified them as advanced. The
computer-anxiety scores of the students were gathered using
Computer Anxiety Rating Scale (CARS; Rosen, Sears & Weil,
1987). The instrument also tried to capture respondents'
computer-anxiety levels with respect to anxiety about the
machines themselves. Demographic questionnaires were
administered to the respondents for finding out information
about respondents' age, sex, ethnic background,
access/ownership of PC, self-ranking of computer competence
etc. The findings reveal that the "advanced" students who
owned PCs were less computer-anxious and revealed more
competence in computer-related tasks. The increased
computer-competence among them were attributable to private

53

experimentation with their home PCs.

Thus, the variable *computer-ownership (O/NO)* is implied to have a two-fold relationship with the variable *computer-anxiety*, with the computer non-owners revealing higher levels of computer-anxiety than owners.

Morrow, Prell and McElroy (1986) are of the opinion that computer-anxious individuals are less likely to own a computer in the near future and therefore continue to suffer from higher levels of computer-anxiety, understandably due to inadequate exposure to computers (Bozinelos, 2004).

Similarly, Ray and Minch's (1990) study suggest that more computer-anxious respondents do not plan to purchase a personal computer in the near future. This is understandable as the respondents who are computer-anxious also report a lesser degree of satisfaction with computers and therefore are less convinced that computers can help them with personal job performances (Thompson, Higgins & Howell, 1991).

The issue of access is particularly important for older users as their age seems to stack against them vis a vis the issue of computer-ownership and access, as historically this group has been found to be more computer-anxious than any other age group.

In support of this fact, studies reveal that the percentage of people accessing computers from their home and the percentage and frequency of such access tend to decrease as the users' ages go up. Data suggest that only 13% of those over 65 years old have used the Internet from their homes, while in the age bracket of 55-64 years 31% have accessed the Web from their home. Twenty-nine percent of Americans in the age group of 65 years or older are able

54

to access computers from their homes, schools, or from other locations occasionally, compared to 71 % of older adults in the age group of 50-64, who are able to access them on a regular basis ("Home Computers and Internet Use in the United States: August 2000," 2001; "Older Americans and the Internet," 2004).

If research findings are taken into consideration, then for older adults, lack of adequate access can qualify as a vital factor affecting their prospects for digital inclusion in less than positive ways, at the same time triggering sustained and spiraling computer-anxiety for the computer users of this age group.

(Computer) *Experience*: A large number of scholars are of the opinion that increasing experience with computer technology works towards diminishing the psychosomatic phenomenon of computer-anxiety (Loyd & Gressard, 1984; Howard & Smith, 1986; Glass & Knight, 1988).

Researchers believe that changes in efficacy that accompany increased (computer) experience have the potential to induce older users to explore advanced technology (Hill, Smith, & Mann, 1987; Kelley et al. 1999). This seems to align with researchers' findings that (computer) experience has the potential of changing the level of user-competence resulting in greater accumulation of knowledge thereby contributing positively to work performances among users (Avoleo, Waldman & McDANIEL, 1990; Salthouse, 1993).

Emery et al. (2003), after examining the effect of combinations of auditory, haptic and/or visual feedbacks on the performance of older adults completing a drag-and-drop computer task under seven feedback conditions (three

unimodal, three bimodal and one trimodal),found that
experienced users responded well to all multi-modal
feedback situations. Twenty-nine volunteer participants of
the study, with a mean age of 73.83 years, who were
recruited for the study based on the criteria of age,
right-handedness, visual acuity, and ocular health, were
assessed using measures of efficiency and accuracy. In a
study conducted with young, middle-aged and older adults,
who learned to use new word processing applications in
keystrokes, menus or menu-plus icons interface conditions,
experienced users revealed age-related slowing in learning
but very few age differences in test performance, when
retrained on a new word processing program. The authors
conclude that the variable (computer) *experience* interacted
with the variable *age* to predict performance (Charness et
al., 2001).

Yang, Mohamed and Beyerbach (1999) conducted a study
on 245 employed vocational technical educators in Dade
County, Florida. Forty-five point five percent of the
participants were male and 54.5 percent were females. About
52.5% of the respondents had completed graduate level
education, about 31.7 % of the respondents had completed
four years of college, and 15.8 % had less than four years
of college education. The data on respondents' computer-
anxiety levels were collected by using a short version of
Computer Anxiety Scale (COMPAS; Oetting, 1983).

The results of the study confirmed that there is an
inverse relationship between computer-anxiety and computer-
competence, with computer-competence stemming from greater
exposure and experience with computers.

Ray and Minch's (1990) study found that the number of

years of (computer) experience is a significant indicator
of the phenomenon of computer-anxiety. For the study
researchers made an effort to construct a theoretically
sound scale that could effectively measure computer users'
anxiety and alienation (a construct used to predict user
reactions to computers). One hundred and fourteen
participants, all undergraduates, were drawn from classes
in which computers were used. The researchers were trying
to measure the construct of computer-anxiety and computer
alienation, somewhat similar constructs, both having
psychological roots in the concept of technological
alienation. Data were gathered using a survey
questionnaire. The study's participants used a Likert-type
scale (Minch & Ray, 1986) that primarily measured
respondents' anxiety and sense of alienation with respect
to computers and their ideas about the impact of the
technology on society and their level of satisfaction with
it. A negative correlation was found to exist between all
the measures and past user experience. It was found that
the truly alienated respondents were less satisfied with
(computer) experience.

Dyck and Smither (1994) conducted a study on 203 older
adults of or over the age of 55 years, and 219 young
adults, age 30 years or younger, who were asked to complete
three instruments which would measure their computer-
attitudes, computer-anxiety and (computer) experience
levels. The researchers discovered that higher levels of
(computer) experience were associated with lower levels of
computer-anxiety among both groups of subjects.
Disability(D/ND): The dichotomous variable *disability(D/ND)*
is implicated to have a two-fold relationship with the
variable *computer-anxiety*; thus a person with disability

has a higher possibility to be computer-anxious than his/her non-disabled counterpart. The literature review suggests that a factor which adversely affects extensive computer use among older adults is disability.

It has been estimated that over one-half of the population in the age group of 65 years or older has disabilities of some sorts. Thirty percent of the people in the age bracket of 50-64 years have at least one of the common disabilities associated with aging, like hearing problems, vision problems, difficulty using hands, walking problems, etc. This figure stands in sharp contrast to people in the younger age groups (people under the 50 years) who are largely free of disabilities. Among the older adults living at home in the year 2002, 26.5 % of the population was found to be suffering from at least some kind of disability, and about 2 million people (6.1% of the population) were found to be severely disabled (Johnson & Wiener, 2006).

The fact is, not only do people from the younger age group (less than 54 years of age) have a lesser probability of having a disability, they are in terms of numerical strength, slightly more than 8 million among the disabled population of the United States (estimated to be around 44 million), which is fewer than one-fifth of the total number of United States' disabled population. On the other hand, the majority of the population who suffer from mobility, vision and hearing-related impairments also tend to fall in the older age group of 65 years or older ("Falling through the Net: Toward Digital Inclusion," 2000; "A Disabled Press," 2000; Russell et al., 1997; Steinmetz, 2006).

The variable *disability* (*D*) hampers Internet usage for disabled users primarily in two ways: first by physically

58

inhibiting individuals' ability to use computer-technology; second, by reducing access for the disabled (along with factors like lower levels of income and education). It is a fact that although computers and operating systems have become increasingly sophisticated, adapting computers for use by people with sensory impairments still remains a major challenge. Disabled people find many websites impossible to access due to poor web navigation capabilities and lack of adaptive hardware and software to access the web. It is estimated that about 78% to 99% of web content is inaccessible to users having some kind disability or impairment.

Also, fewer people with disabilities have any access to computers and the Internet. Only about 24% of Americans with disabilities own a computer as compared to about 52% of their non-disabled counterparts, while only 11% of people with disabilities have Internet access as compared to 31% of their counterparts who are not disabled. About one-quarter of people with some kind of disability, access computers from home as compared to just above one-half of their counterpart who do not suffer from disabilities of any type ("Access to Computers," 2006; "Specific Barriers to Web Access," 1999; "Disability and the Digital Divide," 2007).

Also, a report (2002) entitled "A Nation Online: How Americans Are Expanding their Use of the Internet" claims that about 67.8% of individuals with a disability, who are not employed, are unable to own a computer and are unable to access the Internet on a regular basis. It is interesting that even among the disabled population, employed persons and people with higher education are more likely to own a computer than the unemployed, a fact that is pretty worrisome considering a large percentage of disabled individuals remain without employment all their lives (Kaye, 2000).

Also, the issue of education is important among the disabled population as well in determining access to computers. Due to physical limitations many disabled people are forced to stay away from mainstream education. A large percentage of the population in the older age bracket, who tend to be the most disabled, are out of the tech-savvy group because of economic, educational or disability related reasons. Facing a unique technological barrier, and inhospitable website and technology design, disabled people end up being over-represented among the information-technology have-nots and are more likely to be on the wrong side of the digital divide ("Falling Through the Net: Toward Digital Inclusion," 2000; "Older Americans and the Internet, 2004, "A Nation Online: How Americans Are Expanding their Use of the Internet," 2002).

Though no direct evidence has been found to support the idea that the variable *disability* (*D*) works towards increasing computer-anxiety among disabled users of computer, the author thinks that it is obvious that this group' relative denial of computer access has the potential of robbing the disabled individuals of much needed exposure to computers, thus depriving them of the opportunity to gain experience, self-efficacy, and confidence to use computers (Cassidy & Eachus, 2007).

Table 2.1.identifies studies and the conclusion reached about the way the underlying independent variable *age* aligns with the independent variable *age-related-infirmity*.

Table 2.1. Review of Study Results on relationship between the

Underlying Independent Variables *Age* (UIV) and Independent Variable *Age-Related-Infirmity* (IV)

Variable	Study	Summary Result
		+ (the variable directly affects *Age-Related-Infirmity*) - (the variable inversely affects *Age-Related Infirmity*) **X** (the variable has no affect on *Age-Related-Infirmity*)
Age	• Gietzelt (2001) • *Older people and the Internet* (1997)	• + • +

Similarly, table 2.2. highlights definitive conclusions reached in several studies about how each underlying independent variable purportedly correlates with the independent variable *computer-anxiety*.

Table 2.2. Lit Review of Study Results on relationship between the Underlying Independent Variables (UIVs) and Independent Variable *Computer-Anxiety* (IV)

Variable	Study	Summary Result
		+ (variable directly affects Computer-Anxiety) - (variable inversely affects Computer-Anxiety) X (variable has no affect on Computer-Anxiety)
Age	• Ellis & Allaire (1999) • Laguna & Babcock (1997) • Dyck & Smither (1994) • Butchko (2000)	• + • + • - • X

Table 2.2 —continued

Variable	Study	Summary Result + (variable directly affects Computer-Anxiety) - (variable inversely affects Computer-Anxiety) X (variable has no affect on Computer-Anxiety)
Gender (F)	• Ogozalek (1994) • Durndell & Haag (2002) • Richardson, Zorn & Weaver • Dyck & Smither (1994) • Sam, Othman, & Nordin (2005)	• + • + • + • X • X
Income	• Bozionelos (2004)	• -
Education	• Ellis & Allaire (1999) • Ray & Minch (1990) • Yang, Mohamed, &Beyerbach (1999)	• - • - • -
Computer Ownership (NO)	• Mcinerney, Mcinereney & Sinclair (1990) • Ray & Minch (1990)	• + • +
Experience	• Yang, Mohamed, & Beyerbach (1999) • Dyck & Smither (1994) • Ray & Minch (1990)	• - • - • -
Disability (D)	• Access to Computers (2006) • Specific Barriers to Web Access (1997)	• + • +

To conclude the present chapter primarily reviewed the existing literature in ascertaining how variables like *age*, *gender (M/F)*, *income*, *education*, *computer ownership (O/NO)*, (computer) *experience*, and *disability (D/ND)* relate to *computer-anxiety*, a variable which tends to create barriers for older adult users in access of computer technology.

In this chapter, the author also reviewed the existing literature on how age induced changes in human physiology tend to interfere negatively with the prospect of senior users' access to computer technology. The chapter that follows describes the design of the present research.

METHODOLOGY

The present study tried to explore how *age*, an underlying independent variable is associated with the independent variable *age-related-infirmity (W/WT)*. It also explored the association between each of the underlying independent variables, computer users' 1) *age*, 2) *gender*, 3) *income*, 4) *education*, 5) *computer-ownership (O/NO)*, 6) *experience*, and 7) *disability (D/ND)* status, and the independent variable *computer-anxiety*. Thus the study has seven underlying independent variables (UIVs), in addition to having two independent variables, *age-related-infirmity (W/WT)* and *computer-anxiety* (IVs), which were separately tested for their causal relationships with the dependent variable *barriers-to-computer-use* (DV).

An Analyses of the Study's Variables

The independent variables of the study are of three sub-types: (i) interval level variables include *age*, *income*, *experience, computer-anxiety* and *barriers-to-computer-use*; (ii) categorical-ordinal level variable include *education*; and (iii) categorical (dichotomous) variables include *gender (M/F)*, *disability(D/ND)*, *computer ownership(O/NO)*, *age-related-infirmity(W/WT)*, the latter type seeking participants' responses in terms of two categories "male"/"female" or ""yes/no."

Table 3.1. displays the variables of the study, their types, relationships to other variables, and the statistical tool(s) used to confirm these relationships.

64

Table 3.1. Variable Relationships and Statistical Confirmation

Variable	Type	Affects	Tested By
Age-Related Infirmity (W/WT)	IV (Categorical-Dichotomous)	*Barriers-to-Computer-Use	Independent Samples t test
Age	UIV (Interval)	*Age-Related-Infirmity	Logistic Regression
Computer-Anxiety	IV (Interval)	*Barriers to Computer Use	Pearson's Correlation
Age	UIV (Interval)	*Computer-Anxiety	Pearson's Correlation
Gender (M/F)	UIV (Categorical-Dichotomous)	*Computer-Anxiety	Independent Samples t test
Income	UIV (Interval)	*Computer-Anxiety	Pearson's Correlation
Education	UIV (Ordinal)	*Computer-Anxiety	ANOVA
Computer Ownership (O/NO)	UIV (Categorical-Dichotomous)	*Computer-Anxiety	Independent Samples t test
(Computer) Experience	UIV (Interval)	*Computer-Anxiety	Pearson's Correlation
Disability (D/ND)	UIV (Categorical-Dichotomous)	*Computer-Anxiety	Independent Samples t test

The conceptual framework of the study, also explains the relationships between the study's variables in a fairly graphical manner (for details please refer to Figure 1 in the "Introduction" chapter.

The Methodology for Data Collection

Data Collection: The data for the study was collected through the use of survey questionnaires, an established way for gathering information about individuals' attitudes, beliefs, attributes, opinions and behaviors. Advantages of questionnaires over other methods of data collection include cost savings, participant anonymity and reduced researcher bias ("What is Survey?" 2007; " "Questionnaire Design: General Consideration," 1997; "Advantages of Written Questionnaires," 1997).

Disadvantages of questionnaires include biases if the sampling frame differs significantly from the general population for which the variables are studied. Moreover, biases can be present if the questions serve to influence participants' responses. Finally, surveys can prove to be a difficult method for eliciting responses on sensitive topics like participants' age, income etc. (Kuter & Yilmaz, 2001; Trochim, 2000; Kjeldskov & Graham, 2006)

Sample: The study employed a stratified random sampling technique in selecting potential respondents; the study's sample was comprised of Florida State University's (FSU) permanent employees in the age group of 55 years or older. Stratified random sampling is a commonly employed procedure in social science research for selecting a sample scientifically ("Sampling Methods," 1997).

The population was divided into sub-populations of mutually exclusive units, in this case into two strata containing the academic and non-academic departments from which the prospective participants of the study were chosen. The method of stratification ensured that each stratum containing the target population was proportionately represented in the sample population. The criterion used for such division, was the numerical strength of population unit in the strata. A sample was then drawn separately from each stratum in a random fashion. This was done with a view to increasing the possibility of obtaining an efficient sample, with precise estimates of strata mean. The procedure is also known to enhance the chances of obtaining an accurate estimate of the population mean and other population parameters. Statisticians are of the opinion that lower standard errors and a less biased sample results from this procedure

(Anderson, 1999; Cochran, 1977; "Sampling Strategies and their Advantages and Disadvantages," 2007).

A sample was initially selected from the first of the two strata (Stratum_1) containing FSU's departments with population elements in the magnitude of 1 through ten. This yielded an initial sample consisting of 23 academic and non-academic departments. All the selected departments were contacted and copies of the survey questionnaire, used in this research for data collection purposes, were left with a contact person in the department for prospective participants from the departments thus contacted.

Similarly, a random sample conducted on the second stratum (Stratum_2), containing FSU's academic departments and non-academic departmental entities with population elements of 11 and above yielded a sample of seven academic and non-academic departments. In this case also the academic departments and other non-academic units selected by the sampling procedure were contacted and copies of questionnaires used for the purposes of data gathering (for the present study) were left with department-specific contact persons for distribution among potential respondents.

Several other departments were randomly selected from each stratum from one more round of sampling conducted on the departments and non-departmental entities, as the first round of sampling failed to generate the desired sample size of at least one hundred and twenty. Since the author of this research chose to employ a stratified random sampling procedure without replacement, the next round of sampling from each of the two strata was carried out by eliminating the academic and non-academic departmental units already selected once.

67

The stratification procedure ensured that the
departments both from the first and the second strata had
an equal chances of being selected in the sample.
Stratified random sampling without replacement, as a
strategy, obviated the chances of approaching the same
participants twice (Hunt & Tyrrell, 2004; "Sampling
Techniques," 1995; "Statistical Sampling, Estimation and
Testing," 2001, Trochim, 2006).

The Variables of the Study

Dependent Variable

Barriers-to-computer-use : *Barriers-to-computer-use* is the
final response variable for the study. For the purpose of
this study barrier scores were collected using Inherent
Limitations of Systems and Web Design Scale (ILWDS;
Bhattacharjee, 2006), a 5-point Likert-type scale, with
higher scores indicating more barriers experienced by
respondents in accessing and using computer technology from
the perspective of older users.

The literature review confirmed the presence of two
predictor variables for the dependent variable, *barriers-
to-computer-use; age-related-infirmity* (*W/WT*) and *computer-
anxiety* (Williamson, Bow, & Wale, 1997; Richardson, Zorn, &
Weaver, 2005; Mcilroy, Sadler & Boojawon, 2007; Anthony,
Clarke & Anderson, 2000).

Independent Variable

1.*Age-Related-Infirmity(W/WT)* – The variable *age-related-
infirmity* (*W/WT*) is known to inversely affect successful
computer use for older adult users; because advancing age
destroys the facilities which enables users to interact
smoothly with computers(Zajicek,2001). For example,

68

infirmities related with old age like stiffening of joints and weak musculoskeletal systems have been known to interfere with older adult users' ability to manipulate key computer devices, like the mouse and keyboard. Also, infirmities which are known to inversely affect computer usage among the older adults include problems with vision (Smith & Gove, 2006; Gietzelt 2001), dexterity (Hanson, 2001, Hawthorn, 2000; Charness, Bosman & Elliot, 1995; Worden et al. 1997), cognition (Hanson, 2001; Gleick, 1999; Czaja, 1996; Czaja, 1997; Zajicek, 2001; Zaphiris & Kurniawan, 2001), and hearing (Hanson, 2001).

Underlying Independent Variable

Age- The literature review suggested that *age* is directly related to the independent variable *age-related-infirmity (W/WT)*, meaning that as a person's age goes up the chances of contracting an infirmity rises commensurate with his/her increasing age (Zajicek, 2007; Whitcomb, 2007; Czaja, 2007; Laux, McNally, Paciello & Vanderheiden, 2007).

Independent Variable

2. *Computer Anxiety* - Research suggests that *computer-anxiety*, which is a feeling of anxiety toward the computer, impedes users' chances to interact with the technology of computers to the fullest possible extent, since it leads to a decreased use and avoidance of computer technology (Orr, 2006). Computer-anxiety, as a factor, has been associated with the avoidance and decreased use of computer technology. Howard, Murphy and Thomas (1986) contend that computer-anxiety manifests through a fear of interaction with the computer disproportionate to the threat actually posed by the former. Stated otherwise, computer-anxiety is

a common emotional response to computers marked by explicit fear on the part of many adults.

Underlying Independent Variables

Age - *Age* is an important variable that affects older adult users' interaction with the computers. Research suggests a positive or direct relationship between the variables *age* and *computer-anxiety*; meaning as age of an user go up so does his/her level of computer-anxiety. In support of this fact it can be said that while the overall computer-ownership among people in the age group of 55-75 years is only 30%, as per latest estimates, only 23% percent of the senior citizens over the age of 75 years own a PC (Teel, 2005).

Also, older adults seem to have a declining share of the Internet market. A study conducted by the Pew Internet and American Life Project reveals that while a total of 56% of Americans go online, only about 15% of Americans who are above the age of 65 years has access to the World Wide Web. The same study affirms that only six percent of people over the age of 65 years reported that they plan to go online (Fox, 2004). Many research studies have been able to establish a direct linear correlation between the variables *age* and *computer-anxiety* (viz.: Laguna & Babcock, 1997; Dyck and Smither, 1994; Ellis & Allaire, 1999; Yang, Mohamed & Bayerbach, 1999).

Gender (M/F) -Researchers in general have identified that gender differences are associated with computer use. Older women are less likely than their male counterparts to own computers and to go online (Adler 1995; Timmerman 1998). Older women also report more fear of the technology of computer than their male counterparts. The types of fear

70

they experience range from fear of the machine, fear of the unknown to lack of self confidence (Richardson, Zorn, & Weaver, 2005).

Durndell and Haag (2002) also identify (using undergraduates with an average age of 21.5 years) a relationship between the variable *gender (M/F)* and *computer-anxiety* suggesting that females suffer more from computer-anxiety than males. Despite these findings, other works comparing gender did not identify differences in computer self-efficacy, computer-anxiety, or attitude toward the Internet (Sam, Othman, & Nordin, 2005) based on users' gender stautus.

The present research, however, intended to examine the widely suggested two-fold relationship between the variable *gender (M/F)* and *computer-anxiety*, with a view to validate or refute the assumption that a man suffers significantly less from computer-anxiety than his equivalent female counterpart among the older adult user population.

Income- The variable *income* is associated with a pattern and quality of interaction with computers for the older adult users of computers. The study suggests that people in higher socioeconomic status are more likely to access and use computers and hence suffer less from computer-anxiety (Bozionelos, 2004).

Education - Another variable known to negatively affect older users' computer-anxiety levels is the variable *education*. Among older adults, both the prospect of owning a computer and the likelihood of online participation are related to the level of one's education and other indicators of one's socioeconomic status in general. Some researchers are of the opinion that the variable *education* is a prime determinant of the variable *computer-anxiety*. It

71

is thought that education helps users by lending a
dimension of self-efficacy, and some research even
recommend that higher levels of computer-anxiety can be
substantially altered by boosting self efficacy through
additional training and education (Ellis & Allaire, 1999;
Yang, Mohamed & Beyerbach, 1999; Dyck & Smither 1994,
Doyle, Stamouli, & Huggard, 2005, Bozionelos, 2004).
Computer-Ownership(O/NO): The literature review suggested a
two-fold relationship between the dichotomous variable
computer-ownership(O/NO) and the variable *computer-anxiety*.
The variable *computer-anxiety* is known to affect the
prospect of future ownership of computers, as more
computer-anxious users are likely to stay away from
purchasing a computer. Thus it can be assumed that a
computer owner suffers significantly less from computer-
anxiety than his/her counterpart who does not own a
computer (Ray & Minch, 1990; Morrow, Prell & McElroy,
1986).

(Computer)*Experience*- Ray and Minch report a study which
examined the relationship between the variables *computer-
anxiety* and *experience* ("Computer Anxiety and Alienation:
Toward a Definitive and Parsimonious Measure," 1990). The
results of the study indicated that the number of years of
(computer) experience is a significant indicator of the
magnitude of computer-anxiety experienced by a user. Other
research has also found that higher levels of (computer)
experience were associated with lower levels of computer-
anxiety (Dyck & Smither, 1994)

Disability (D/ND)[1] – The literature review implied that this
variable shares a two-fold relationship with the construct
computer anxiety. Charness and Holley (2004) confirmed that
people with disabilities are less likely to have computer
access, and it seems that this might be the reason behind
the higher prevalence of computer-anxiety among the
disabled users. Less computer access translates to less
computer usage, and a lower sense of self efficacy among
disabled computer users leading to higher levels of
computer-anxiety among them (Beckers & Smith, 2003; Higgins
& Howell, 1994).

**Table 3.2. The variables of the study including their measurement
points, scales and the basis for using them.**

Variable	Type/General Description	Measurement Question/Instrument	Basis
Barriers-to-computer-use	The interval-level dependent variable Data gathered with a 5-point Likert -type questionnaire	Questionnaire ILSWDS (Inherent Limitations of Systems and Web Design Scale; Bhattacharjee,2006)	• Mcilroy, Sadler,& Boojawon (2007) • Dunn, Hoppin, and Wendt (1999) • Williamson • Bow,& Wale(1997)
A ge-Related-Infirmity (W/WT)	A categorical dichotomous independent variable Data gathered with a single question	Do you think this (disability/disabilities) is/are a part of the general process of aging (arising from such age-related incidents as arthritis, cancer, stroke etc.)? Yes No	• Smith & Gove, (2006) • Hanson (2001) • Hawthorn (2000) • Williamson Bow& Wale(1997)

---

[1] For the purpose of this research we are using the definition of disability suggested by
the American Disabilities Act (ADA, 1990) as a person a) with a physical or mental
impairment, which substantially limits a major life activity; b) who has a record or
history of such an impairment; and, c) who is regarded as having such an impairment.

Table 3.2 —continued

Variable	Type/General Description	Measurement Question/Instrument	Basis
Age	An interval-level underlying independent variable Data gathered with a single question	Your age (in years): Under 55 55-64 65-74 75 and above	• Kurniawan & Zaphiris (2007)
Computer-Anxiety	An interval-level independent variable Data gathered with a 5-point Likert-type questionnaire	Questionnaire MCAS (Modified Computer Anxiety Scale; Bhattacharjee, 2006)	• Cohen & Waugh (1989) • Maki & Maki (2007)
Age	An interval-level underlying independent variable Data gathered with a question	Your age (in years): Under 55 55-64 65-74 75 and above	• Laguna & Babcock (1997) • Ellis & Allaire (1999)
Gender (M/F)	A categorical dichotomous underlying independent variable Data gathered with a question	Your gender status: Male Female	• Durndell and Haag (2002)
Income	An interval-level underlying independent variable Data gathered with a question	Your income (To the nearest 1000 US Dollars): Under 30,000 30,000-40,000 40,000-50,000 50,000-60,000 60,000 and Above	• Bozionelos (2004).
Education	An ordinal underlying independent variable Data gathered with a question	The most recent degree you have attained (No certificates or diplomas please): High School Associate Bachelors Master's Specialist Ph.D.	• Ellis & Allaire (1999) • Yang (1999)
Computer-Ownership (O/NO)	Categorical dichotomous underlying independent variable Data gathered with a question	Do you have a personal computer at home? Yes No	• Mcinerney, Mcinerney & Sinclair (1990) • Ray & Minch

Table 3.2 —continued

Variable	Type/General Description	Measurement Question/Instrument	Basis
Experience	Interval-level underlying independent variable Data gathered with a question	Years of computing experience you have (To the nearest whole number in year/s)? Below ½ year ½ year -1 year 1 year- 2 years 2years -3 years 3 years - 4years 4 years -5 years 5 years and Above	• Ray & Minch (1990) • Dyck and Smither (1994)
Disability (D/ND)	Categorical dichotomous underlying independent variable Data gathered with a question	Do you suffer from any disabilities? Yes No	• Access to Computers (2006) • Specific Barriers to Web Access, (1997)

The Instruments of the Study

The First Questionnaire

The study used three questionnaire, for collecting data for the study. The first questionnaire (or instrument) address the construct of computer anxiety using a scale fashioned after Computer Anxiety Scale (CAS; Cohen & Waugh, 1989). CAS (1989) is a 16 -item self-report inventory, which assesses respondents' comfort level with computers, and is scored from 1 to 5 (the lowest possible computer anxiety score for this instrument is 16 and the highest possible score is 80), with higher scores indicating greater anxiety. The instrument CAS (1989), has been used as an example for questionnaire design for the present study with the idea that the scale assesses users' reactions to computers via the construct computer-anxiety in a reliable manner and is one of the best validated

75

measures of computer-anxiety, with a high internal
consistency reflected by an alpha coefficient of .936.

The scale was first used by Cohen and Waugh (1989) to
assess the construct of computer-anxiety among 43 graduate
psychology students and 109 undergraduate psychology
students. The scale, then a 20-item questionnaire with an
alpha of .936, was subsequently reduced to a 16-item
instrument with an alpha coefficient of .948.

The scale was administered by Maki and Maki (2003) to
ascertain respondents' level of comfort with computers
among a total of 544 university students over a 2-year
period (1999-2001). The respondents completed both the web-
based and face-to-face versions of a class, with a view
towards helping to demonstrate as to how individual
characteristics of students can result in varying levels of
learning satisfaction in web-based classes as opposed to
face-to-face lecture sessions. The scale was also used in
other studies, including Brown & Coney's (1994) research
for determining the magnitude of computer-anxiety among 51
medical interns (average age 27 years) and their attitude
towards medical computer applications.

For the purposes of the present study, however,
questions 2 & 12 in Cohen & Waugh's CAS (1989) were
reworded and question 15 was dropped as it was thought to
be redundant. This produced the Modified Computer Anxiety
Scale (MCAS; Bhattacharjee, 2006), a 15-item 5-point
Likert-type questionnaire (the fifteenth question being the
same as the sixteenth question used in the original CAS
(1989). Respondents' scoring options ranged from "Strongly
Agree" (5) to "Strongly Disagree" (1). The researcher
devised the scoring key of the MCAS (2006) along the lines
of CAS (1989) by reverse coding the negatively worded

items. Like CAS (1989), the scoring option for the MCAS (2006) ranged from "Strongly Agree" (5) to "Strongly Disagree" (1). However, unlike CAS (1989), the total maximum attainable points on this scale is 75 and the total minimum points attainable on this scale is fifteen.

Following CAS (1989), the scale was coded by reversing the scores on the scale's positively worded statements, questions 3, 8, 9, 10, 13 and fifteen.

The Second Questionnaire

The second of the three-part questionnaire (also an instrument for data collection), identified as Inherent Limitations of Systems and Web Design Scale (ILSWDS; Bonny Bhattacharjee, 2006), consists of a Likert-type scale, with response options ranging from "Strongly Agree" to "Strongly Disagree," on a 5-point scale. The scale was designed to measure the degree of constraints experienced by older users in relation to features like the mouse, keyboard, menus, scrolling bars, blinking texts, color of websites, navigation bars, error recovery features etc., and was devised by the researcher in accordance with the findings of the literature review. The 19-questions of the instrument aim to find out the extent to which older users' deteriorating visual, auditory, cognitive, bone, joint, and muscular faculties affect web interaction for senior users.

The questionnaire seeks to find out the degree to which features like color, font sizes, font types, lengthy text, patterned backgrounds, etc., affect older users' failing vision and create constraints in web navigation. The questions attempt to assess the extent to which web-related features like blinking texts, scrolling texts, background noise etc., affect the declining cognitive and deficient attention structures of older users in defining the process of successful manipulation of computers for older adult users. Also, the questions are geared towards assessing the impact of features like navigation bars, site maps, and error recovery provisions on older users' poor navigational skills, which partially arise due to their limited spatial memory resources. Other questions were designed to evaluate the degree of influence older users' poor mouse and keyboard manipulation abilities have on the ability to navigate the web effectively, therefore underscoring the role a senior users' declining musculoskeletal system play in web navigation. One question purported to measure the extent of influence multimedia features like sound have on older users' diminished auditory capabilities, in an attempt to determine the degree to which this affects the potential of effective interaction with computers.

The questionnaire contains two positively worded statements (questions 13 and 18) and 17 negatively worded statements (all other questions). For each question respondents offered their responses on a 5-point Likert-type scale, with their options ranging from "Strongly Agree" (5) to "Strongly Disagree" (1). The maximum attainable points on this instrument is 95 and the minimum obtainable points on this scale is nineteen.

The total barrier-score of each respondent, was assessed by reverse scoring the positive statements. The only question requiring a text response was worded, "Do you think you have anything else to share with us about your computer/Internet experience?" the question was designed to record any other constraints that the questionnaire did not identify.

An extensive review of the literature (as stated below) provided the theoretical basis for the construction of the above instrument. Research revealed that older users of computer technology possess unique physical, sensory, and cognitive features (working memory, attentional processes, and spatial cognition), which erect significant barriers to their use of the Internet and other computer technologies. It is thus imperative that designers of interfaces make every effort to accommodate older users affected by age-related infirmities to a more conducive web environment by ameliorating the limitations imposed by their faltering physical, sensory and cognitive characteristics (Zajicek, 2007; Czaja, 2007; Laux, McNally, Paciello & Vanderheiden, 2007).

The scale tried to represent four basic constructs centered around the faculties identified as vulnerable to infirmities in older adults and corresponding design solutions for addressing the computer performances barriers they give rise to:

The Vision Factor

Researchers have proved that older adult users with poor eye sight require larger on screen texts (Mayhew, 1992). Bernard, Liao & Mills (2001) found out through a study conducted on 27 older adults, with their ages ranging from 62 to 83, that 14-point fonts promote more legibility, faster reading and were preferred to 12-point fonts by the users trying to read contents from the web.

Physical spacing is important with respect to laying out the content of the text for sites meant for older adults. By using the white spaces (the spaces between letters, words and lines) efficiently, the designer can come up with a page that is easy to read. Blocks of text with insufficient leading may appear too crowded to an older user who has limited peripheral vision. This problem may be solved by increasing the leading by 1 or 2 points and by avoiding condensed typefaces and by increasing the space between letters (Holt, 2000; "Older Adults and the World Wide Web," 1999).

Web pages need to be organized in such a way so that each item is discussed and dealt with at length before moving on to the next item, as most older adults tend to perform better if they accomplish one task before moving on to another. This necessitates that if a lengthy document is being presented, it should be broken up into smaller, clearly distinguishable sections (Park, 1992; "Older Adults and the World Wide Web," 1999). Precise and effective labeling can aid in organizing the material to be read, and brevity in documentation is required as short documents make retrieval of facts easier for the user (Hartley, 1994; Morrow & Leirer, 1999).

Similarly, it is also important to make sure that there is plenty of contrast between the background and the text. It is good from a usability standpoint to make sure that dark graphics or text is displayed against a light background (Echt, 2002; "Making Your Web Site Senior Friendly," 2004).

It is advisable that web designers avoid a patterned background. This is because even with contrast, the pattern in the background can adversely affect the impact of the text in the foreground thereby impairing ease of reading among older adult users (Holt, 2000).

The Cognitive Factor

It is advisable to keep the length the of web sites short in order to spare older adults the task of extensive scrolling. It has been suggested that short web pages require less scrolling and thus tend to facilitate web navigation for older adults (Morrell, Dailey, & Rousseau, 2003).

Care should be taken about not including automatically scrolling texts in web sites, as that impairs older adults' ability to read contents of the sites at his or her own speed -thereby interfering with hassle-free comprehension among older users who have slower reading and word recognition speed. If manual scrolling is a requirement then it should be ensured that specific scrolling icons are incorporated in each page (Holt, 2000; Holt & Morrell, 2002; "Making Your Web Site Senior Friendly," 2004).

It is advisable that for documents running into a couple of pages there should be a provision for a navigation bar at the top of each page so that the users can quickly get to the item they are looking for. Also there should be a secondary menu to aid proper navigation of the document. It has been proven that carefully labeled links and navigational tools ease the task of navigation for users (AgeLight LCC, 2001; Holt & Morrell, 2002; "Older Adults and the World Wide Web," 1999).

Also site maps have been proven to be very effective in helping older navigators to determine where they are on a site with respect to other pages. This gives them a sense of direction about how to navigate to other pages in the site (Westerman, et al., 1995).

Older users retain more text-based information if it comes embedded with animated graphics or videos. However, animated graphics and videos should always be accompanied by text, or a text only option version should be provided to those users whose computers cannot download animations ("Older Adults and the World Wide Web," 1999).

In order to minimize the element of distraction among older adult users, efforts should be made to cut down on features like blinking texts, flashing lights or animation in constant motion (Holt, 2000).

The Musculo-Skeletal Factor

It was found that older adults prefer a traditional menu over a pull down menu. Poor mouse coordination and lack of exact movements, which pull down menus require, have the potential of impeding senior users' ability to use this screen control (Rogres & Fisk, 2004; Noyes & Sheard, 2003).

Also, it is important to enhance the accessibility of web sites for the benefit of older adults; therefore the number of clicks necessary for accessing information should be kept at a minimum. This is because many of the older adults have less than perfect motor skills which hinder effective manipulation of mouse (Walker, Millians & Worden, 1996).

The Auditory Factor

Similarly, if audio is used it must be used with corresponding text alternatives. If translated to its design equivalents it does mean that a text version of the audio is made available as an alternative to the video and animations used on the web site. The addition of these features is assumed to decrease working memory demands of older adults (Morrell, Dailey & Rousseau, 2003; Morrell, Mayhorn & Echt, 1996, 1997; Morrell, Mayhorn & Bennett, 2002).

The Third Questionnaire

The third of the three-part questionnaire contains questions aimed at eliciting information from respondents on focal variables like *age*, *gender (M/F)*, *income*, *education*, *computer-ownership*, (computer) *experiences*, *disability (D/ND)*, and *age-related-infirmity (W/WT)* status of the respondents. The questions in this questionnaire are either multiple choice questions, to which the respondents' answered by ticking an appropriate category from among many categories (for variables *age*, *income*, *education*, *experience*), or to which the respondents recorded their feedback by selecting "yes"/ "no," "male"/"female," type responses -for variables such as *gender (M/F)*, *computer-ownership (O/NO)*, *disability (D/ND)*, and *age-related-infirmity (W/WT)*.

Responses for two peripheral variables *area of work* and *job designation* were sought by asking participants to tick against appropriate types from among categories like "faculty"/"staff;" "humanities"/"social sciences"/ "science+ tech"/and "other" etc.

Details of the Study Execution

The study was administered at Florida State University's Tallahassee campus, in the state of Florida. The sampling frame consisted of permanent employees of Florida State University's multiple academic and non-academic departments, aged 55 years or older.

A stratified random sampling procedure was followed

for selecting the participants for the study. FSU's (Florida State University) academic and non-academic entities like College of Music, Department of Political Science, Department of Physics, Department of Dance, and non-academic departments like International Programs, Office of Technology Integration, Department of Business Services, Building Services to name a few, comprised the pool from which the academic departments and non-academic entities were selected (Reazin, personal communication, April 16, 2006).

The departments were arranged in strata with reference to their relative strengths (based on prior information), in terms of the population elements they contain. Each stratum thus did not contain equal numbers of academic departments or non-academic departmental entities. The academic departments and non-academic departmental entities were aggregated in two strata (Stratum_1 and Stratum _2), and were selected in a random fashion. For stratum number one (Stratum_1), which was known to contain academic and non-academic departments, with older adult employee populations ranging from 1 through 10, the sampling procedure yielded a total of 23 departments containing elements from the targeted population.

Similarly, academic and non-academic departments were selected from stratum number two (Stratum_2), in a random fashion following the procedure of simple random sampling. Seven academic/non-academic departments were selected in this fashion.

About 25% of the academic/ non-academic departments refused to participate in the study so the process of random sampling was carried out in both strata until a targeted sample size of 121 participants was reached.

A person (representatives such as administrative assistants/secretaries) was contacted from each selected department, either by the researcher herself or by her research assistant. Questionnaires were left with those who were contacted, for distribution among the permanent employees (belonging to the concerned departments).

During the initial contact sessions, the secretaries/administrative assistants of the selected departments were apprised about the study-related details and were requested to distribute copies of the questionnaires and informed consent forms (which stated that the survey was only directed at respondents who are 55 years or older) among the faculty and non-faculty permanent employees of their departments. Finally, the researcher and her assistant left the departments with assurances that they would return in a week to pick up the completed questionnaires.

According to instructions (in the informed consent form) the participants were requested to return the completed questionnaires to the researcher or her assistant via media the contact person in each department, within the specified time frame of one week. Accordingly, the researcher or her assistant returned within the specified seven days period to collect the returned questionnaires.

The number of questionnaires which were finally returned amounted to one hundred and forty. However, five of them were discarded because respondents were below 55 years of age, and 14 of them had to be destroyed because of fear of data replication (as they could not be separated from a questionnaire stack from which data had already been entered in the data editor). This left a total sample size of one hundred and twenty -one.

Through the consent form the participants were introduced to such study-related details as the topic of the study, the significance of the research, the number and types of questions which would be posed in each part of the three part questionnaire, and the total number of questions they will be required to respond to.

Participants were also informed about the approximate time they would need to fill out each part of the questionnaire. The respondents were made aware of the potential risks, benefits, and demands associated with the study. The participants were assured that they would emerge anonymous from the study, as their responses would be identified with reference to codes assigned against their names on the questionnaire they have filled out.

On the participants' end, each participant was requested to sign the informed consent form and return it along with the completed questionnaires to their respective departmental secretaries or to the person who handed them the instruments/questionnaires. At the end of the survey, the completed questionnaires and the informed consent forms were collected from the qualified participants (within the specified period of seven days) by the people who administered the questionnaires, for the purpose of analyses.

In all, it was the intention of the author to present in this chapter, a feasible design for the research, which in retrospect enabled her to collect data for the study in a precise fashion. The information generated from the data collected was utilized towards providing accurate answers to the study's research questions and hypotheses. The following chapter discuses in detail, the statistical tools, which were employed to analyze the data gleaned, the

data analyses process, and the conclusions reached through
such analyses.

DATA ANALYSIS

The statistical analysis for the study was
accomplished through the employment of the following : (1)
binary logistic regression, for determining whether a
single interval level predictor variable is significant for
a regression model that has single dichotomous dependent
variable; (2) one-way ANOVA, used for determining any
significant differences between three and more mutually
exclusive categories, divided by an ordinal (with three or
more levels) grouping (independent) variable, vis a vis an
interval level test (dependent) variable. If the means of
the groups did not vary in a significant manner it was
concluded that the independent variable did not affect the
dependent variable; (3) the correlation co-efficient
Pearson's R, was used to measure the direction and
magnitude of association between two interval level
variables. Independent samples t test was used as a special
case of ANOVA, for unraveling any existing significant
difference between two mutually exclusive categories -
divided by a dichotomous grouping (independent) variable;
vis a vis an interval level test (dependent) variable. The
t tests were carried out with the assumption that the
variances of the different groups were unequal (Garson,
2007; Howell, 1998; ANOVA, 1999; "SPSS for Windows:
Descriptive and Inferential Statistics," 2007; Garson,
1998).

Table 4.1. The Variables and the Statistical Tools Used to Determine the Nature of their Relationships

Nature of Independent Variable	Nature of Dependent Variable	The Tests
Continuous (Interval)	Categorical (Dichotomous)	Logistic Regression
Continuous (Interval)	Continuous (Interval)	Correlation (Pearson's R)
Categorical (Ordinal/Dichotomous)	Continuous (Interval)	One-way ANOVA/independent samples t test

*The Basics of Statistical Analysis, 2007

As stated earlier, for the purpose of the study dichotomous (binary) and ordinal (with three or more levels) variables were deemed as categorical variables, and interval level variables were deemed as continuous variables. The variable *education*, for example, depicted in terms of degrees earned in sequential order, was regarded as an ordinal hence a categorical variable; ANOVA was thus rightfully used as a statistical test to measure its level of association with its interval level outcome variable *computer-anxiety* (Newsom, 2007; "An Overview: Choosing the Correct Statistical Test," 2007).

Data Coding and Recoding

To ease the process of data analysis the variable (computer) *experience*, represented by question 6c (recd6) and the variable *area of work* represented by question 13c (recd13c) were recoded, for two different reasons. The variable (computer) *experience* was recoded to equalize the categories against which the respondents had offered their responses, and the variable *area of work* was recoded in order to convert a string variable, with which the responses were collected, into a numeric variable. The

89

computer-anxiety score (anxiety_score) representing the variables *computer-anxiety* and the barriers-to-computer-use score (barrier_score) representing the variable *barriers-to-computer-use*, were each recoded into scorea and scoreb respectively in three categories of 1, 2, and 3 by dividing the original interval level scales into three equal parts, sequentially ordered in an ascending order from 1 through 3 with higher scores in both scales indicating more computer-anxiety and more barriers faced in interacting with computers (Newsom, 2007; "An Overview: Choosing the Correct Statistical Test," 2007).

The dichotomous variables of the study, requiring "yes,"/ "no" types of responses were coded into categories of 1 and 0, with 1 representing "yes" and 0 representing "no." The variable *gender* with two levels *male* and *female* (*M/F*) were coded in two categories with 1 representing "female" and 0 representing "male".

A Brief Introduction to the Demographics of the Sampled Respondents

The following questions were culled from the only demographic questionnaire designed for this study. Each question aided in gathering information about important variables like *age*, *gender (M/F)*, *income*, *education*, (computer) *experience*, *computer-ownership* (O/NO), *disability* (*D/ND*), and *age-related-infirmity* (*W/WT*) status of the study's respondents.

The data thus provided were analyzed with SPSS to help depict the respondents' response patterns, bar-charts were used to graphically represent the data supplied by the respondents.

Questions 8C and 10C of the demographic questionnaire were omitted from data analysis because of the nature of variables (string variables) they represent.

1C. Your age (In years):

Under 55 -----------------

55-64   ---------------------

65-74 ---------------------

75 and Above----------------

Table 4.2. Table to Assess Response on Question 1C

Ques1C

		Frequency	Percent	Valid Percent	Cumulative Percent
Valid	55-64	110	90.9	90.9	90.9
	65-74	10	8.3	8.3	99.2
	75 and above	1	.8	.8	100.0
	Total	121	100.0	100.0	

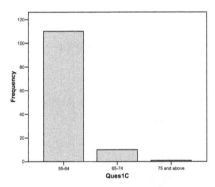

Figure 2.A Bar Chart Representing the Age of the Respondents

2C.Your gender status: Male ------------------------

Female----------------------

Table 4.3. Table to Assess Response on Question 2C

Ques2C

		Frequenc y	Percent	Valid Percent	Cumulative Percent
Vali d	Male	58	47.9	47.9	47.9
	Female	63	52.1	52.1	100.0
	Total	121	100.0	100.0	

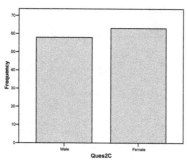

Ques2C

Figure 3.A Bar Chart Representing the Gender Status of the Respondents

3C. Your income (To the nearest thousand in dollars):

Under 30,000 -------------------

30, 000-40,000 ------------------

40,000-50,000--------------------

50,000-60,000---------------------

60,000 and Above----------------

Table 4.4. Table to Assess Response on Question 3C

Ques3C

		Frequency	Percent	Valid Percent	Cumulative Percent
Valid	Under 30,000	21	17.4	17.6	17.6
	30, 000-40,000	24	19.8	20.2	37.8
	40,000-50,000	19	15.7	16.0	53.8
	50,000-60,00	12	9.9	10.1	63.9
	60,000 and above	43	35.5	36.1	100.0
	Total	119	98.3	100.0	
Missing	System	2	1.7		
Total		121	100.0		

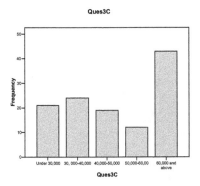

Ques3C

Figure 4.A Bar Chart Representing the Income of the Respondents

4C. The most recent degree you have attained (No
certificates or diplomas, please):

High School ----------------

Associate -------------------

Bachelors--------------------

Master's---------------------

Specialist--------------------

Ph.D.------------------------

93

Table 4.5. Table to Assess Response on Question 4C

Ques4C

		Freque ncy	Percen t	Valid Percent	Cumulati ve Percent
Valid	High School	32	26.4	27.1	27.1
	Associ ate	17	14.0	14.4	41.5
	Bachel ors	21	17.4	17.8	59.3
	Master 's	21	17.4	17.8	77.1
	Specia list	5	4.1	4.2	81.4
	Ph.D.	22	18.2	18.6	100.0
	Total	118	97.5	100.0	
Missin g	System	3	2.5		
Total		121	100.0		

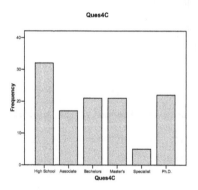

Figure 5.A Bar Chart Representing the Educational Status of the Respondents

5C. Do you have a personal computer at home? Yes ----------
-------No----------------------

Table 4.6. Table to Assess Response on Question 5C

Ques5C

		Frequency	Percent	Valid Percent	Cumulative Percent
Valid	No	13	10.7	10.7	10.7
	Yes	108	89.3	89.3	100.0
	Total	121	100.0	100.0	

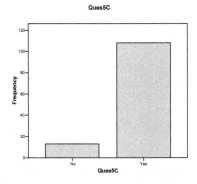

Figure 6.A Bar Chart Representing the Computer Ownership Status of the Respondents

6C. Years of computing experience you have (To the nearest whole number, in year/s)? :

Below ½ year

½ year -1 year

1year- 2 years

2-years -3 years

3 years – 4years

4 years -5 years

5 years and Above

Table 4.7. Table to Assess Response on Question Recd6C

recd6

		Frequency	Percent	Valid Percent	Cumulative Percent
Valid	1.00	4	3.3	3.3	3.3
	2.00	1	.8	.8	4.1
	4.00	1	.8	.8	5.0
	6.00	115	95.0	95.0	100.0
	Total	121	100.0	100.0	

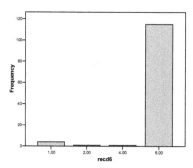

recd6

Figure 7.A Bar Chart Representing the Computer Experience Level of the Respondents

7C.Do you suffer from any disability/disabilities? (Yes) -- ------------- (No) --------------

Table 4.8. Table to Assess Response on Question 7C

ues7C

		Frequency	Percent	Valid Percent	Cumulative Percent
Valid	No	103	85.1	85.1	85.1
	Yes	18	14.9	14.9	100.0
	Total	121	100.0	100.0	

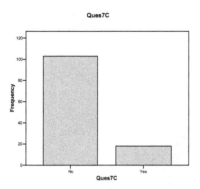

Figure 8.A Bar Chart Representing the Number of Respondents Who Reported Having Disabilities

9C. Is it /are these disability/disabilities congenital (from birth)? (<u>Answer</u> this question <u>only if</u> you have <u>answered question # 8</u>): (Yes)---------- (No)---------------

Table 4.9. Table to Assess Response on Question 9C

Ques9C

		Frequency	Percent	Valid Percent	Cumulative Percent
Valid	No	14	11.6	82.4	82.4
	yes	3	2.5	17.6	100.0
	Total	17	14.0	100.0	
Missing	System	104	86.0		
Total		121	100.0		

97

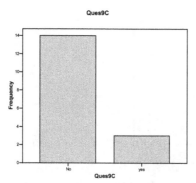

Ques9C

Figure 9.A Bar Chart Representing the Number of Respondents Who Reported Having Congenital Disabilities

11C. Do you think this (disability/disabilities) is/are a part of the general process of aging (arising from such age-related incidents as arthritis, cancer, stroke etc.)? (Please <u>answer</u> this question <u>only if</u> you have answered <u>question # 10</u>): (Yes)..............................(No) ....

Table 4.10. Table to Assess Response on Question 11C

		Frequency	Percent	Valid Percent	Cumulative Percent
Valid	No	8	6.6	50.0	50.0
	Yes	8	6.6	50.0	100.0
	Total	16	13.2	100.0	
Missing	System	105	86.8		
Total		121	100.0		

Ques11C

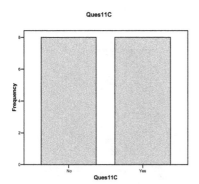

Ques11C

Figure 10.A Bar Chart Representing the Number of Respondents Who Reported Having Age-Related-Infirmities

12C. What is your job designation?   Faculty -------- Staff ------------

Table 4.11. Table to Assess Response on Question 12C

Ques12C

		Frequency	Percent	Valid Percent	Cumulative Percent
Valid	Faculty	27	22.3	22.9	22.9
	Staff	91	75.2	77.1	100.0
	Total	118	97.5	100.0	
Missing	System	3	2.5		
Total		121	100.0		

99

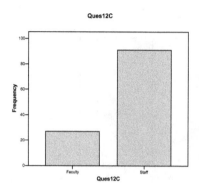

Figure 11.A Bar Chart Representing the Job Designation Status of the Respondents

13C. The people you work with are primarily involved with (circle one): Humanities ------- Social Sciences ------------- Science+ Tech ----------------------- Other ------------------ (Administration, Professional, Support Staff etc)

Table 4.12. Table to Assess Response on Question 13C

Recd13

		Frequency	Percent	Valid Percent	Cumulative Percent
Valid	1.00	10	8.3	9.3	9.3
	2.00	15	12.4	13.9	23.1
	3.00	23	19.0	21.3	44.4
	4.00	60	49.6	55.6	100.0
	Total	108	89.3	100.0	
Missing	System	13	10.7		
Total		121	100.0		

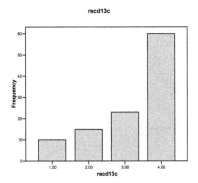

recd13c

Figure 12.A Bar Chart Representing the Area of Work of the Respondents

A Discussion on the Study's Demographic Details

The demographic questionnaire helped seek answers to some crucial questions about the socio-economic and demographic background of the participants of this study. They are as follows:

Age: One hundred and ten respondents (90.9%) were in the age category 55-64. There was only one respondent from the age group 75 and above, who constituted 0.8% of the total respondents. The age group 65-74 contained 10 respondents constituting about 8.3% of the total population.

Gender Status (M/F): Fifty-eight males (47.9%) and 63 (52.1%) females participated in the present study, to make up 121 valid participants.

Income: About 53.8% of the respondents had an income which ranged from under $30,000 to $ 50,000 annually. About 10.1% of the respondents grossed between $ 50,000 to $ 60,000 annually and about 36.1% of the population had an annual income of $ 60, 0000 and above. Two respondents did not report their income levels.

101

Education: Majority (27.1%) of the respondents had a High School degree, and about 18.6% of the participants had a Ph.D. degree. Three respondents did not report the degrees they attained.

Computer-Ownership (O/NO): Out of a total of 121 respondents only 13 people -10.7% of the respondents did not own a personal computer, as opposed to 108 (89.3%) respondents who reported having a personal computer.

(Computer) Experience: About 115 (95%) respondents out of a total of 121 respondents had an experience of 5 years and above, as opposed to only 4 (3.3%) respondents having an experience of less than 1 year to 1 year. This is amazing, it implicates that the study was executed among a very computer-literate population.

Disability (D/ND): A total of 17 people reported having some kind of disability but only 3 people reported having congenital disabilities (from birth). This was about 17.6 (valid) percent of the respondent population.

The disabilities reported by the respondents were arthritis, neck injury, spinal cord impairment, myopia, deafness in the ear, amputated arm etc.

Age-Related-Infirmity (W/WT): Only 8 participants reported having some kind of infirmities associated with old age. The other 8 respondents who reported having some kind of infirmities did not think that their infirmities were age-related.

Job Designation: A total of 27 people or 22.3% of the respondents were faculty members, and also 91 (75.2%) of non-faculty employees took part in the survey. Three or 2.5% of the respondents did not specify their designations.

Area of Work: Ten people, 9.3% (valid) of the respondents who participated in the survey, were working in areas

related to humanities. Fifteen, 13.9% (valid) of the
respondents, were from social sciences domain, 23 or 21.3%
(valid) of the respondents, were listed as being from
science and technology related areas, and 60 or
55.6%(valid) of the data, came from administrative,
professional and support-staff members from non-academic
areas. Thirteen respondents did not report any specifics
regarding their work areas.

Research Questions

The research was driven by a set of research
questions, as follows:

1. Does the variable *gender (M/F)* have a two-fold
relationship with the variable *computer-anxiety*, for older
adult users of the computer?

2. Is there a relationship between *computer-anxiety* on the
one hand and each of the demographic variables, *income*,
education, and (computer) *experience*, on the other?

3. Does the dichotomous variable *computer-ownership (O/NO)*
have a two-fold relationship with the variable *computer-
anxiety?*

4. Does the variable *disability (D/ND)* relate to *computer-
anxiety* in a dichotomous fashion?

5. Does the demographic variable *age* affect the variable
computer-anxiety in a direct fashion?

Answers to the Research Questions

According to the order established for the
variables, in the series of research questions, each
variable was tested for a relationship with its
corresponding response variable through the appropriate
procedure.

1. Does the variable *gender (M/F)* have a two-fold
relationship with the variable *computer-anxiety*, for older
adult users of the computer?

Table 4.13. (a & b): An Independent Samples t test: *Gender* and
Computer Anxiety

Table: 4.13 a

Group Statistics

	Ques2C	N	Mean	Std. Deviation	Std. Error Mean
scorea	Male	54	1.6111	.62696	.0853
	Female	63	1.6190	.55150	.0694

Independent Samples Test
t-test for Equality of Means

Table: 4.13 b

		Levene's Test for Equality of Variances					
		F	Sig.	T	df	Sig. (2-tailed)	Mean Difference
scorea	Equal variances assumed	1.692	.196	-.073	115	.942	-.00794
	Equal variances not assumed			-.072	106.550	.943	-.00794

An independent samples t test was run to measure how each
gender type, *male*, *female (M/F)*, influences the variable
computer-anxiety. The significance value for the above test
=.942 is greater than alpha=.05. Therefore, the researcher
failed to reject the null hypothesis and concluded that
there is no difference in the mean of computer-anxiety in

104

the two categories of *gender (M/F)*, t (115)=-.073, p=.942. Thus it was construed that the variable *gender (M/F)* does not seem to have an effect on the computer-anxiety level of an individual (Archambault, 2000), for this study's population.

2.Is there a relationship between *computer-anxiety* on the one hand and each of the demographic variables, *income*, *education*, and (computer) *experience*, on the other?

Table 4.14. Correlation: *Income* and *Computer-Anxiety* Correlations

		Ques3C	scorea
Ques3C	Pearson Correlation	1	-.272
	Sig. (2-tailed)		.003
	N	119	115
scorea	Pearson Correlation	-.272	1
	Sig. (2-tailed)	.003	
	N	115	117

The researcher tried to determine the nature of relationship between the interval-level variables *income* and *computer-anxiety* by running a bivariate correlation procedure.

The negative correlation coefficient (-.272) indicated that there is a statistically significant (p= .003 < alpha= .05) relationship between a respondents' income level and his /her computer-anxiety level. The negative relationship between these two variables is one in which the value of one variable increases as the other decreases. Therefore, the researcher concluded that that when an individual's income goes up by one unit his/her computer- anxiety level, represented by computer-anxiety score (scorea) goes down by

.272 unit ("SPSS for Windows: Descriptive and Inferential Statistics," 2007).

Table 4.15. (a & b): **ANOVA**: *Education* and *Computer-Anxiety*

Table: 4.15 a

Descriptives

scorea

	N	Mean	Std. Deviation	Std. Error	Minimum	Maximum
High School	31	1.6129	.49514	.08893	1.00	2.00
Associate	17	1.7647	.56230	.13638	1.00	3.00
Bachelors	20	1.7000	.47016	.10513	1.00	2.00
Master's	21	1.4286	.59761	.13041	1.00	3.00
Specialist	5	1.8000	.44721	.20000	1.00	2.00
Ph.D.	20	1.3500	.58714	.13129	1.00	3.00
Total	114	1.5789	.54683	.05122	1.00	3.00

Table 4.15 b

ANOVA

scorea

	Sum of Squares	df	Mean Square	F	Sig.
Between Groups	2.683	5	.537	1.863	.107
Within Groups	31.107	108	.288		
Total	33.789	113			

A one-way ANOVA was run using SPSS (Statistical Package for the Social Sciences), with the ordinal variable *education* and the interval-level variable *computer-anxiety*, to determine the effect of the predictor variable *education* on its corresponding response variable *computer-anxiety*. We compared the mean level of computer-anxiety of the High School, Associate, Bachelor's, Master's, Specialist and PhD degree holders. It would appear that the Specialists (M=1.8000) have the highest mean level of computer-anxiety and the PhDs (M=1.3500) have the lowest mean level of computer-anxiety. The p value for the F test is not significant (.107> alpha= .05); therefore it was construed that no significant difference exists between the two

106

groups on the results of one-way ANOVA. The researcher concluded that no significant difference exist among the six categories of education on their levels of computer-anxiety. In other words, an F statistic that is not significant indicates that the variable *education* does not affect the variable *computer-anxiety* (Archambault, 2000).

Table 4.16. Correlation: (Computer) *Experience* and *Computer-Anxiety*

Correlations

		recd6	scorea
recd6	Pearson Correlation	1	-.371
	Sig. (2-tailed)		.000
	N	121	117
scorea	Pearson Correlation	-.371	1
	Sig. (2-tailed)	.000	
	N	117	117

The researcher tried to determine the nature of relationship between the interval-level variables (computer) *experience*, and *computer-anxiety* by running a bivariate correlation procedure.

The negative Pearson correlation coefficient (-.371) indicated that there is a statistically significant (*p* =.000 < .05) relationship between a respondents' experience level with computers and his /her computer-anxiety level. The negative relationship between these two variables is one in which the value of one variable increases as the other decreases. Therefore, the researcher concluded that, for this population, when an individual's (computer) experience level goes up by one unit his /her computer-anxiety level (scorea) goes down by .371 unit ("SPSS for Windows: Descriptive and Inferential Statistics," 2007).

107

3. Does the dichotomous variable *computer ownership (O/NO)* have a two-fold relationship with the variable *computer-anxiety?*

Table 4.17. (a & b): An Independent Samples t test: *Computer Ownership (O/NO)* and *Computer-Anxiety*

Table 4.17:a

Group Statistics

	Ques5C	N	Mean	Std. Deviation	Std. Error Mean
scorea	No	13	2.1538	.68874	.19102
	Yes	104	1.5481	.53752	.05271

Independent Samples Test
t-test for Equality of Means

Table 4.17:b

		Levene's Test for Equality of Variances					Mean
		F	Sig.	t	df	Sig. (2-tailed)	Difference
scorea	Equal variances assumed	.006	.940	3.709	115	.000	.60577
	Equal variances not assumed			3.057	13.887	.009	.60577

An independent samples t test was conducted to determine the effect of the dichotomous variable *computer-ownership (O/NO)* on the variable *computer-anxiety* (scorea).

The independent samples t test analysis indicated that the 13 respondents without computers had a mean score of 2.1538 in MCAS (Modified Computer Anxiety Scale; Bhattacharjee, 2006), and 104 respondents with computers had a mean score of 1.5481 total in MCAS (Modified Computer

108

Anxiety Scale; Bhattacharjee, 2006). Thus the means did differ significantly at the p<.05 level (note: p = .000) and the observed difference in the means (.6057) is significant. Since the output implicated that the observed difference in the means is significant {t (115) = -.3.709, p=.000}, the researcher rejected the null hypothesis and concluded that the means of the two groups are significantly different; and a significant increase in computer-anxiety occurred in the *computer-ownership* (*NO*) group compared to the *computer-ownership* (*O*) group (Price, 2000).

4. Does the variable *disability (D/ND)* relate to *computer-anxiety* in a dichotomous fashion?

Table 4.18. (a & b): An Independent Samples t test: *Disability Status (D/ND)* and *Computer-Anxiety*
Table: 4.18a

Group Statistics

	Ques9C	N	Mean	Std. Deviation	Std. Error Mean
scorea	No	14	1.5000	.51887	.13868
	yes	3	1.3333	.57735	.33333

Table: 4.18b

Independent Samples Test
t-test for Equality of Means

		Levene's Test for Equality of Variances					
		F	Sig.	t	df	Sig. (2-tailed)	Mean Differenc e
scorea	Equal variances assumed	1.544	.233	.497	15	.626	.16667
	Equal variances not assumed			.462	2.740	.678	.16667

An independent samples t test was run using SPSS (Statistical Package for the Social Sciences) to determine the effect of the dichotomous variable *disability (D/ND)* on the interval variable *computer-anxiety*. The significance value for the test is .626 which is greater than the alpha = .05. Therefore, the researcher failed to reject the null hypothesis and concluded that there is no difference in the mean of computer-anxiety (scorea) in the two categories of *disability (D/ND)*, t(15)=.497, p=.626. Thus the variable *disability (D/ND)* does not seem to have an effect on the computer-anxiety level of an individual for this population (Archambault, 2000).

5. Does the demographic variable *age* affect the variable *computer-anxiety* in a direct fashion?

Table 4.19. Correlation: *Age* and *Computer-Anxiety*

Correlations

		Ques1C	scorea
Ques1C	Pearson Correlation	1	.025
	Sig. (2-tailed)		.786
	N	121	117
scorea	Pearson Correlation	.025	1
	Sig. (2-tailed)	.786	
	N	117	117

The researcher tried to determine the nature of relationship between the interval-level variables *age* and the variable *computer-anxiety* by running a bivariate correlation procedure.

The Pearson correlation coefficient (.025) indicated that there is no statistically significant (p =.786 >.05)

110

relationship between a respondents' age and his /her level of computer-anxiety for this population.

Hypotheses Tests

H1. The variable *age* has a two-fold relationship with the variable *age-related-infirmity* (W/WT).

Table 4.20. (a, b & c): Logistic Regression: *Age* and *Age-Related-Infirmity* (W/WT)

Table 4.20 a

Case Processing Summary

Unweighted Cases(a)		N	Percent
Selected Cases	Included in Analysis	16	13.2
	Missing Cases	105	86.8
	Total	121	100.0
Unselected Cases		0	.0
Total		121	100.0

a If weight is in effect, see classification table for the total number of cases.

Table 4.20 b

Classification Table(a)

			Predicted		
			Ques11C		Percentage Correct
Observed			No	Yes	
Step 1	Ques11C	No	0	8	.0
		Yes	0	8	100.0
	Overall Percentage				50.0

a. The cut value is .500

Table 4.20c

Variables in the Equation

		B	S.E.	Wald	df	Sig.	Exp(B)
Step 1(a)	Ques1C	.000	1.155	.000	1	1.000	1.000
	Constant	.000	2.646	.000	1	1.000	1.000

a Variable(s) entered on step 1: Ques1C.

111

A logistic regression was run with the categorical dichotomous variable *age-related-infirmity* (*W/WT*) as the dependent variable and the interval-level variable *age* as the predictor variable. The output provided information on (i) goodness of fit for the model (ii) and goodness of fit of the predictor variable.

The predictor variable did not appear to be significant for our regression model (p=1.000> alpha=.05). Thus the researcher concluded that variable *age* appears to be a bad predictor of whether an individual has age-associated infirmities or not. Thus it can be said with certainty that the variable *age* does not have any association with the variable *age-related-infirmity* ("Statistics," 2007).

The researcher is of the opinion that an older individual does not suffer more from infirmities compared to his/her equivalent younger counterpart for this population. The hypothesized (H1) effect of the variable *age* on the variable *age-related-infirmity* (*W/WT*) was thereby not confirmed.

H2.There is a direct linear relationship between the variable *computer-anxiety* and the variable *barriers-to-computer-use*.

Table 4.21. Correlation: *Computer-Anxiety* and *Barriers-to-Use*

Correlations

		scorea	scoreb
scorea	Pearson Correlation	1	.313
	Sig. (2-tailed)		.001
	N	117	111
scoreb	Pearson Correlation	.313	1
	Sig. (2-tailed)	.001	
	N	111	114

The researcher tried to determine the nature of relationship between the variables *computer-anxiety* and *barriers-to-computer-use*, both interval-level variables, by running a bivariate correlation procedure.

The positive Pearson correlation coefficient (.313) indicated that there is a statistically significant (p=.001 < .05) direct linear relationship between a respondent's computer-anxiety score (scorea) level and his /her barriers-to-computer-use score (scoreb) level. The direct linear relationship between these two variables is one in which the value of one variable increases as the other increases. Therefore, the researcher concluded that that when the computer-anxiety level (scorea) of a respondent goes up by one unit his/her barriers-to-computer-use level (scoreb) goes up by .313 unit ("SPSS for Windows: Descriptive and Inferential Statistics," 2007).

Thus a rise in the level of computer-anxiety is accompanied by a rise in the level of barriers faced by users, in access and manipulation of computer technology. The hypothesized (H2) relationship between the variables *computer-anxiety* and the variable *barriers-to-computer-use* was thereby confirmed.

H3.The variable *age-related-infirmity (W/WT)* has a two-fold relationship with the dependent variable *barriers-to-computer-use*.

Table 4.22. (a & b): An Independent Samples T test: *Age-related-Infirmity (W/WT)* and *Barriers-to-Computer-Use*

Table 4.22 a

Group Statistics

	Ques11C	N	Mean	Std. Deviation	Std. Error Mean
scoreb	No	7	2.1429	.37796	.14286
	Yes	8	2.3750	.51755	.18298

Table 4.22 —continued

Table 4.22 b

Independent Samples Test

		Levene's Test for Equality of Variances					
		F	Sig.	t	df	Sig. (2-tailed)	Mean Difference
scoreb	Equal variances assumed	4.386	.056	-.978	13	.346	-.23214
	Equal variances not assumed			-1.000	12.651	.336	-.23214

An independent samples t test was conducted using SPSS (Statistical Package for the Social Sciences), to find out how the dichotomous variable *age-related -infirmity (W/WT)*, affects its interval-level response variable *barriers-to-computer-use*. The significance value for the above test is .346 and is greater than alpha=. 05. Therefore, the researcher failed to reject the null hypothesis and concluded that there is no difference in the mean of barriers-to-computer-use levels in the two categories of the variable *age-related-infirmity (W/WT)*, t (13) = -.978, p=.346. Thus the variable *age-related-infirmity (W/WT)* did not seem to have an effect on the level of barriers faced by individual users in using and accessing computer technology for this population (Archambault, 2000).

The researcher concluded that an individual with one or more infirmities associated with old age does not suffer from greater magnitude of barriers in trying to access and manipulate computer technology compared to his/her

114

equivalent counterpart who does not suffer from such associated infirmities.The hypothesized (H3) dichotomous relationship between the variable *age-related-infirmity* (*W/WT*) and the variable *barriers-to-computer-use* was thereby not confirmed.

Findings: The Peripheral Variables

Table 4.23. (a & b): An Independent Samples T test: *Job Designation* and *Computer-Anxiety*

Table: 4.23a

Group Statistics

	Ques12C	N	Mean	Std. Deviation	Std. Error Mean
scorea	Faculty	25	1.4000	.57735	.11547
	Staff	89	1.6629	.56294	.05967

Table 4.23b

Independent Samples Test
t-test for Equality of Means

		Levene's Test for Equality of Variances					
		F	Sig.	t	df	Sig. (2-tailed)	Mean Difference
scorea	Equal variances assumed	.010	.920	-2.052	112	.043	-.26292
	Equal variances not assumed			-2.023	37.795	.050	-.26292

An independent samples t test was conducted to determine whether the ordinal variable *job designation* affects a respondent's computer-anxiety level. The

115

independent-sample t test analysis indicated that the 25
faculty members had a mean score of 1.4000 in MCAS, and 89
staff members had a mean score of 1.6629 total in MCAS, the
means did differ significantly at the p<.05 level (note: p
= .043). Thus the observed difference in the means (-.2629)
is significant. Since the output implicated that the
observed difference in the means is significant {t (112) =
-.2.052, p=.043}, the researcher rejected the null
hypothesis and concluded that the means of the two groups
are significantly different, and a significant increase in
computer-anxiety occurred in the non-faculty employee group
compared to the faculty group for this population (Price,
2000).

Table 4.24. (a, b, c & d): ANOVA: *Area of Work* and *Computer-Anxiety*

Table: 4.24a

Descriptives

scorea

	N	Mean	Std. Deviation	Std. Error
1.00	10	1.6000	.69921	.22111
2.00	15	1.3333	.48795	.12599
3.00	21	1.4286	.50709	.11066
4.00	58	1.7759	.59362	.07795
Total	104	1.6250	.59427	.05827

Table 4.24 b

ANOVA

scorea

	Sum of Squares	df	Mean Square	F	Sig.
Between Groups	3.413	3	1.138	3.451	.019
Within Groups	32.962	100	.330		
Total	36.375	103			

A one-way ANOVA was run using SPSS (Statistical
Package for the Social Sciences) to measure how Florida

116

State University's employees' area of work affects their
computer-anxiety levels (scorea). The p value for the F
test is significant, .019 < alpha level at .05. Therefore
we concluded that a significant difference exist within
comparisons of computer-anxiety levels among the four area
of work categories (e.g., humanities, social sciences,
science+ tech, other -administration, professional, and
support staff).In other words a significant F statistic
tells us that employees' area of work has a significant
effect on the levels of computer-anxiety (scorea)
experienced by them. Thus the researcher concluded that the
variables *computer-anxiety* and *area of work* are related.

Table: 4.24c

Post Hoc Tests
Multiple Comparisons

Dependent Variable: scorea
Tukey HSD

(I) recd13c	(J) recd13c	Mean Difference (I-J)	Std. Error	Sig.	95% Confidence Interval	
					Lower Bound	Upper Bound
1.00	2.00	.26667	.23439	.667	-.3457	.8791
	3.00	.17143	.22059	.865	-.4049	.7478
	4.00	-.17586	.19658	.808	-.6895	.3378
2.00	1.00	-.26667	.23439	.667	-.8791	.3457
	3.00	-.09524	.19409	.961	-.6024	.4119
	4.00	-.44253(*)	.16631	.044	-.8770	-.0080
3.00	1.00	-.17143	.22059	.865	-.7478	.4049
	2.00	.09524	.19409	.961	-.4119	.6024
	4.00	-.34729	.14622	.089	-.7293	.0347
4.00	1.00	.17586	.19658	.808	-.3378	.6895
	2.00	.44253(*)	.16631	.044	.0080	.8770
	3.00	.34729	.14622	.089	-.0347	.7293

*   The mean difference is significant at the .05 level.

Table 4.24 d

Homogeneous Subsets
Scorea

Tukey HSD

Table 4.24d —continued

recd13 c	N	Subset for alpha = .05
		1
2.00	15	1.3333
3.00	21	1.4286
1.00	10	1.6000
4.00	58	1.7759
Sig.		.113

Means for groups in homogeneous subsets are displayed.
a. Uses Harmonic Mean Sample Size = 17.277.
b. The group sizes are unequal. The harmonic mean of the group sizes is used.
Type I error levels are not guaranteed.

The SPSS (Statistical Package for the Social Sciences) yielded 12 pairwise comparisons. The value of the difference between the group means is stated here, along with the significance of each comparison. SPSS (Statistical Package for the Social Sciences) adjusted for the multiple pairwise comparisons using Tukey's HSD, so one can take these significance levels as they are listed.

There are significant differences between group 4 and group 2, and group 2 and group 4 in both cases group 4 being superior ("Psych 218- Third SPSS Tutorial Multiple Comparisons," 2000).

Data Analysis: Discussion

In the aftermath of the data analyses the following results emerged:

1. It was found that no significant relationship/ association exists between the variables *computer-anxiety* and *gender (M/F)*, which means that a *male* is not significantly less computer anxious than his equivalent *female* counterpart, for this population.

2. *Income*, as a variable was found to be significantly related with the variable *computer-anxiety*, in a negative

118

fashion. The result of the correlation analysis and the direction of correlation coefficient Pearson's R endorsed this conclusion. Thus we can say that when a person's income (in 1000 US dollars) goes up, his/her computer anxiety level goes down and vice-versa, ignoring all other variables for this population.

Education, an ordinal level variable was not found to be significantly related/ associated with the interval-level variable *computer-anxiety*. This was confirmed by the results of the ANOVA analysis. Thus it can be said that a person's level of education has no impact on the level of computer-anxiety he or she experiences for this population.

Experience (with computers), an interval-level variable, was found to be significantly associated, in a negative fashion, with interval-level variable *computer-anxiety*. The result of the correlation analysis, and the magnitude and direction of the correlation coefficient Pearson's R, proved this conclusion. Thus as a respondents' (computer) experience goes up (in years), his/her level of computer-anxiety goes down and vice-versa, ignoring all other variables for this population.

3. The dichotomous variable *computer-ownership* (*O/NO*) was found to be significantly related with the interval-level variable *computer-anxiety* in a dichotomous fashion. Thus a person who owns a computer is likely to suffer less from computer-anxiety than his/her equivalent who does not own a computer for this population.

4. *Disability (D/ND)* the categorical-dichotomous variable was not found to have any association with the variable *computer-anxiety* for this population. The results of the independent sample t test helped the researcher arrive at this conclusion. Thus we can say a person's disability

119

status has no impact on the level of computer-anxiety
he/she experiences; thus a person with disability will
experience the same level of computer-anxiety as that of an
equivalent, without disability.
5. *Age*, an interval variable, was not found to have any
significant association with the variable *computer-anxiety*.
The results of correlation analysis lent credence to this
fact. Thus it was surmised that a respondent's age has no
significant influence on his/her level of computer-anxiety
for this population. Thus an aged person is likely to
suffer from the same level of computer-anxiety as that of
his younger counterpart, ignoring all other variables.

The categorical-dichotomous variable *job designation*
was found to have a significant relationship with the
variable *computer-anxiety*, as confirmed by the results of
the independent samples t-test. Thus we can say with
certainty that a person's work position - whether or not a
respondent is a faculty or staff member, plays a role in
determining his/her level of computer-anxiety. In the
context of the present study the difference in computer-
anxiety level were significant between the faculty and the
staff members in favor of the former-meaning the faculty
member suffered from significantly lower levels of
computer-anxiety compared to the staff members for this
population.

The output from the ANOVA analysis also revealed the
existence of a significant relationship between the ordinal
variable *area of work* and the interval-level variable
computer-anxiety. The difference was found to be
significant between group 2 (Social Sciences) and group 4
(others-administrative, professional and support staff),
with the former experiencing significantly lower levels of

120

computer-anxiety compared to the latter. Thus the researcher concluded that a respondent's area of work predict his/her level of computer-anxiety for this population.

The results of the Hypotheses tests:

H1: The interval-level variable *age* was not found to have any relationship/association with the dichotomous variable *age-related-infirmity (W/WT)*; the results of the logistic regression analysis helped endorse this conclusion. Thus we failed to prove the fact that age is an apt predictor of the extent of infirmities an individual suffers from.

H2: The independent variable, *computer-anxiety* was found to have significant relationship with the dependent variable of the study, *barriers-to-computer-use*, this was borne out by the results of the correlation analysis. Thus the researcher concluded that as a respondent's level of computer-anxiety (indicated by scorea) goes up, the barrier level (indicated by scoreb) faced by him/her in accessing the technology of computer tends to go up as well.

Thus the researcher was successful in establishing the hypothesized fact that the interval-level independent variables *computer-anxiety* and *barriers-to-computer-use* are directly related.

H3: The categorical-dichotomous independent variable, *age-related-infirmity (W/WT)* was found to have no significant relationship/association with the dependent variable, *barriers-to-computer-use*. The conclusion was endorsed by the results of independent samples t test analyses.

Thus, the researcher failed to conclude that a person who suffers from infirmities associated with old age faces a significantly higher level of barrier in using and accessing computer technology than an equivalent person without such infirmities.

Frequency Counts

Also a frequency test was run in SPSS to find out the exact number of people (also corresponding percentages) who answered the Likert-type questionnaires, in "strongly disagree'" "disagree," "neutral," "agree," "strongly agree," mode for each question in the above-mentioned questionnaires. The following tables display the findings:

Q 1A-I feel anxious whenever I am using computers.

Table: 4.25. Table to Assess Response on Question 1A

Ques1A

		Frequency	Percent	Valid Percent	Cumulative Percent
Valid	Strongly Disagree	59	48.8	49.2	49.2
	Disagree	39	32.2	32.5	81.7
	Neutral	12	9.9	10.0	91.7
	Agree	3	2.5	2.5	94.2
	Strongly Agree	7	5.8	5.8	100.0
	Total	120	99.2	100.0	
Missing	System	1	.8		
Total		121	100.0		

Q 2A-I am nervous when I sit down at the computer.

Table 4.26. Table to Assess Response on Question 2A

Ques2A

		Frequency	Percent	Valid Percent	Cumulative Percent
Valid	Strongly Disagree	69	57.0	57.5	57.5
	Disagree	39	32.2	32.5	90.0
	Neutral	6	5.0	5.0	95.0
	Agree	2	1.7	1.7	96.7
	Strongly Agree	4	3.3	3.3	100.0
	Total	120	99.2	100.0	
Missing	System	1	.8		

Table 4.26 —continued

	Frequency	Percent	Valid Percent	Cumulative Percent
Total	121	100.0		

Q 3A- I am confident in my ability to use computers.

Table 4.27. Table to Assess Response on Question 3A

Ques3A

		Frequency	Percent	Valid Percent	Cumulative Percent
Valid	Strongly Disagree	13	10.7	10.7	10.7
	Disagree	13	10.7	10.7	21.5
	Neutral	12	9.9	9.9	31.4
	Agree	38	31.4	31.4	62.8
	Strongly Agree	45	37.2	37.2	100.0
	Total	121	100.0	100.0	

Q 4A-I feel tense whenever working on a computer.

Table 4.28. Table to Assess Response on Question 4A

Ques4A

		Frequency	Percent	Valid Percent	Cumulative Percent
Valid	Strongly Disagree	60	49.6	49.6	49.6
	Disagree	41	33.9	33.9	83.5
	Neutral	10	8.3	8.3	91.7
	Agree	4	3.3	3.3	95.0
	Strongly Agree	6	5.0	5.0	100.0
	Total	121	100.0	100.0	

Q 5A-I worry about making mistakes on the computer.

Table 4.29. Table to Assess Response on Question 5A

Ques5A

		Frequency	Percent	Valid Percent	Cumulative Percent
Valid	Strongly Disagree	52	43.0	43.0	43.0
	Disagree	36	29.8	29.8	72.7
	Neutral	17	14.0	14.0	86.8
	Agree	10	8.3	8.3	95.0

123

Table 4.29 —continued

	Frequency	Percent	Valid Percent	Cumulative Percent
Strongly Agree	6	5.0	5.0	100.0
Total	121	100.0	100.0	

Q 6A- I try to avoid using computers whenever possible.

Table 4.30. Table to Assess Response on Question 6A

Ques6A

		Frequency	Percent	Valid Percent	Cumulative Percent
Valid	Strongly Disagree	82	67.8	67.8	67.8
	Disagree	25	20.7	20.7	88.4
	Neutral	3	2.5	2.5	90.9
	Agree	7	5.8	5.8	96.7
	Strongly Agree	4	3.3	3.3	100.0
	Total	121	100.0	100.0	

Q 7A- I experience anxiety whenever I sit in front of a computer terminal.

Table 4.31. Table to Assess Response on Question 7A

Ques7A

		Frequency	Percent	Valid Percent	Cumulative Percent
Valid	Strongly Disagree	66	54.5	55.0	55.0
	Disagree	40	33.1	33.3	88.3
	Neutral	4	3.3	3.3	91.7
	Agree	4	3.3	3.3	95.0
	Strongly Agree	6	5.0	5.0	100.0
	Total	120	99.2	100.0	
Missing	System	1	.8		
Total		121	100.0		

Q 8A-I enjoy working with computers.

Table 4.32. Table to Assess Response on Question 8A

Ques8A

		Frequency	Percent	Valid Percent	Cumulative Percent
Valid	Strongly Disagree	4	3.3	3.4	3.4
	Disagree	4	3.3	3.4	6.7
	Neutral	15	12.4	12.6	19.3
	Agree	47	38.8	39.5	58.8
	Strongly Agree	49	40.5	41.2	100.0
	Total	119	98.3	100.0	
Missing	System	2	1.7		
Total		121	100.0		

Q 9A-I would like to continue working with computers in the future.

Table 4.33. Table to Assess Response on Question 9A

Ques9A

		Frequency	Percent	Valid Percent	Cumulative Percent
Valid	Strongly Disagree	2	1.7	1.7	1.7
	Disagree	3	2.5	2.5	4.2
	Neutral	11	9.1	9.2	13.3
	Agree	45	37.2	37.5	50.8
	Strongly Agree	59	48.8	49.2	100.0
	Total	120	99.2	100.0	
Missing	System	1	.8		
Total		121	100.0		

Q 10A -I feel relaxed when I am working on a computer.

Table 4.34. Table to Assess Response on Question 10A

Ques10A

		Frequency	Percent	Valid Percent	Cumulative Percent
Valid	Strongly Disagree	4	3.3	3.3	3.3
	Disagree	8	6.6	6.6	9.9
	Neutral	22	18.2	18.2	28.1
	Agree	43	35.5	35.5	63.6

Table 4.34 —continued

	Frequency	Percent	Valid Percent	Cumulative Percent
Strongly Agree	44	36.4	36.4	100.0
Total	121	100.0	100.0	

Q 11A- I wish that computers were not as important as they are.

Table 4.35. Table to Assess Response on Question 11A
Ques11A

		Frequency	Percent	Valid Percent	Cumulative Percent
Valid	Strongly Disagree	25	20.7	20.7	20.7
	Disagree	32	26.4	26.4	47.1
	Neutral	28	23.1	23.1	70.2
	Agree	27	22.3	22.3	92.6
	Strongly Agree	9	7.4	7.4	100.0
	Total	121	100.0	100.0	

Q 12A-Computers frighten me.

Table 4.36. Table to Assess Response on Question 12A

Ques12A

		Frequency	Percent	Valid Percent	Cumulative Percent
Valid	Strongly Disagree	69	57.0	57.0	57.0
	Disagree	33	27.3	27.3	84.3
	Neutral	7	5.8	5.8	90.1
	Agree	5	4.1	4.1	94.2
	Strongly Agree	7	5.8	5.8	100.0
	Total	121	100.0	100.0	

Q 13A-I feel content when I am working on a computer.

Table 4.37. Table to Assess Response on Question 13A

Ques13A

		Frequency	Percent	Valid Percent	Cumulative Percent
Valid	Strongly Disagree	5	4.1	4.1	4.1

126

Table 4.37 —continued

	Frequency	Percent	Valid Percent	Cumulative Percent
Disagree	7	5.8	5.8	9.9
Neutral	37	30.6	30.6	40.5
Agree	46	38.0	38.0	78.5
Strongly Agree	26	21.5	21.5	100.0
Total	121	100.0	100.0	

Q 14A -I feel overwhelmed when I am working on a computer.

Table 4.38. Table to Assess Response on Question 14A

Ques14A

		Frequency	Percent	Valid Percent	Cumulative Percent
Valid	Strongly Disagree	61	50.4	50.4	50.4
	Disagree	37	30.6	30.6	81.0
	Neutral	11	9.1	9.1	90.1
	Agree	6	5.0	5.0	95.0
	Strongly Agree	6	5.0	5.0	100.0
	Total	121	100.0	100.0	

Q 15A- I feel at ease with computers.

Table 4.39. Table to Assess Response on Question 15A

Ques15A

		Frequency	Percent	Valid Percent	Cumulative Percent
Valid	Strongly Disagree	7	5.8	5.8	5.8
	Disagree	6	5.0	5.0	10.7
	Neutral	15	12.4	12.4	23.1
	Agree	50	41.3	41.3	64.5
	Strongly Agree	43	35.5	35.5	100.0
	Total	121	100.0	100.0	

Q 1B- I have difficulty reading a text size smaller than 14-point on the screen.

Table 4.40. Table to Assess Response on Question 1B

Ques1B

		Frequency	Percent	Valid Percent	Cumulative Percent
Valid	Strongly Disagree	30	24.8	25.2	25.2
	Disagree	42	34.7	35.3	60.5
	Neutral	19	15.7	16.0	76.5
	Agree	22	18.2	18.5	95.0
	Strongly Agree	6	5.0	5.0	100.0
	Total	119	98.3	100.0	
Missing	System	2	1.7		
Total		121	100.0		

Q 2B- I prefer computer texts that are neither very big nor very small.

Table 4.41. Table to Assess Response on Question 2B

Ques2B

		Frequency	Percent	Valid Percent	Cumulative Percent
Valid	Strongly Disagree	1	.8	.8	.8
	Disagree	7	5.8	5.8	6.6
	Neutral	23	19.0	19.0	25.6
	Agree	74	61.2	61.2	86.8
	Strongly Agree	16	13.2	13.2	100.0
	Total	121	100.0	100.0	

Q 3B- I have difficulty reading computer texts that appear too crowded.

Table 4.42. Table to Assess Response on Question 3B

Ques3B

		Frequency	Percent	Valid Percent	Cumulative Percent
Valid	Strongly Disagree	10	8.3	8.3	8.3
	Disagree	21	17.4	17.5	25.8
	Neutral	25	20.7	20.8	46.7
	Agree	55	45.5	45.8	92.5

Table 4.42 —continued

		Frequency	Percent	Valid Percent	Cumulative Percent
	Strongly Agree	9	7.4	7.5	100.0
	Total	120	99.2	100.0	
Missing	System	1	.8		
Total		121	100.0		

Q 4B- I prefer online texts, which appear in clearly identifiable sections.

Table 4.43. Table to Assess Response on Question 4B

		Frequency	Percent	Valid Percent	Cumulative Percent
Valid	Strongly Disagree	1	.8	.8	.8
	Disagree	7	5.8	5.8	6.6
	Neutral	31	25.6	25.6	32.2
	Agree	64	52.9	52.9	85.1
	Strongly Agree	18	14.9	14.9	100.0
	Total	121	100.0	100.0	

Q 5B- I prefer contrast in colors between the background and the text displayed on the screen.

Table 4.44. Table to Assess Response on Question 5B

Ques5B

		Frequency	Percent	Valid Percent	Cumulative Percent
Valid	Disagree	4	3.3	3.3	3.3
	Neutral	33	27.3	27.5	30.8
	Agree	63	52.1	52.5	83.3
	Strongly Agree	20	16.5	16.7	100.0
	Total	120	99.2	100.0	
Missing	System	1	.8		
Total		121	100.0		

Q 6B- I do not prefer patterned backgrounds.

Table 4.45. Table to Assess Response on Question 6B

Ques6B

		Frequency	Percent	Valid Percent	Cumulative Percent
Valid	Strongly Disagree	5	4.1	4.1	4.1
	Disagree	5	4.1	4.1	8.3
	Neutral	38	31.4	31.4	39.7
	Agree	56	46.3	46.3	86.0
	Strongly Agree	17	14.0	14.0	100.0
	Total	121	100.0	100.0	

Q 7B -I think animated graphics and videos should always be accompanied by text.

Table 4.46. Table to Assess Response on Question 7B

Ques7B

		Frequency	Percent	Valid Percent	Cumulative Percent
Valid	Strongly Disagree	6	5.0	5.0	5.0
	Disagree	23	19.0	19.0	24.0
	Neutral	57	47.1	47.1	71.1
	Agree	28	23.1	23.1	94.2
	Strongly Agree	7	5.8	5.8	100.0
	Total	121	100.0	100.0	

Q 8B- I have difficulty dealing with features like blinking texts.

Table 4.47. Table to Assess Response on Question 8B

Ques8B

		Frequency	Percent	Valid Percent	Cumulative Percent
Valid	Strongly Disagree	10	8.3	8.3	8.3
	Disagree	35	28.9	28.9	37.2
	Neutral	36	29.8	29.8	66.9
	Agree	33	27.3	27.3	94.2
	Strongly Agree	7	5.8	5.8	100.0
	Total	121	100.0	100.0	

Q 9B-I have difficulty moving through web sites, which have
automatically scrolling texts.

+

Table 4.48. Table to Assess Response on Question 9B

Ques9B

		Frequency	Percent	Valid Percent	Cumulative Percent
Valid	Strongly Disagree	19	15.7	15.7	15.7
	Disagree	48	39.7	39.7	55.4
	Neutral	24	19.8	19.8	75.2
	Agree	28	23.1	23.1	98.3
	Strongly Agree	2	1.7	1.7	100.0
	Total	121	100.0	100.0	

Q 10B-I have difficulty navigating a site, which does not
have labeled (hyper) links.

Table 4.49. Table to Assess Response on Question 10B

Ques10B

		Frequency	Percent	Valid Percent	Cumulative Percent
Valid	Strongly Disagree	17	14.0	14.0	14.0
	Disagree	44	36.4	36.4	50.4
	Neutral	28	23.1	23.1	73.6
	Agree	29	24.0	24.0	97.5
	Strongly Agree	3	2.5	2.5	100.0
	Total	121	100.0	100.0	

Q 11B- I prefer web sites that have site maps.

Table 4.50. Table to Assess Response on Question 11B

Ques11B

		Frequency	Percent	Valid Percent	Cumulative Percent
Valid	Strongly Disagree	2	1.7	1.7	1.7
	Disagree	11	9.1	9.1	10.7
	Neutral	50	41.3	41.3	52.1

131

Table 4.50 —continued

	Frequency	Percent	Valid Percent	Cumulative Percent
Agree	45	37.2	37.2	89.3
Strongly Agree	13	10.7	10.7	100.0
Total	121	100.0	100.0	

Q-12B I prefer web sites that have clearly visible buttons and icons.

Table 4.51. Table to Assess Response on Question 12B

Ques12B

		Frequency	Percent	Valid Percent	Cumulative Percent
Valid	Strongly Disagree	1	.8	.8	.8
	Disagree	1	.8	.8	1.7
	Neutral	18	14.9	14.9	16.5
	Agree	79	65.3	65.3	81.8
	Strongly Agree	22	18.2	18.2	100.0
	Total	121	100.0	100.0	

Q 13B- I prefer pull down menus, which appears when I select an item with a mouse.

Table 4.52. Table to Assess Response on Question 13B
Ques13B

		Frequency	Percent	Valid Percent	Cumulative Percent
Valid	Strongly Disagree	1	.8	.8	.8
	Disagree	5	4.1	4.1	5.0
	Neutral	41	33.9	33.9	38.8
	Agree	60	49.6	49.6	88.4
	Strongly Agree	14	11.6	11.6	100.0
	Total	121	100.0	100.0	

Q 14B-I prefer websites that are just a mouse click away.

132

Table 4.53. Table to Assess Response on Question 14B

Ques14B

		Frequency	Percent	Valid Percent	Cumulative Percent
Valid	Disagree	1	.8	.8	.8
	Neutral	26	21.5	21.5	22.3
	Agree	73	60.3	60.3	82.6
	Strongly Agree	21	17.4	17.4	100.0
	Total	121	100.0	100.0	

Q 15B-I do not prefer web sites, which require extensive scrolling.

Table 4.54. Table to Assess Response on Question 15B

Ques15B

		Frequency	Percent	Valid Percent	Cumulative Percent
Valid	Strongly Disagree	3	2.5	2.5	2.5
	Disagree	6	5.0	5.0	7.4
	Neutral	35	28.9	28.9	36.4
	Agree	59	48.8	48.8	85.1
	Strongly Agree	18	14.9	14.9	100.0
	Total	121	100.0	100.0	

Q 16B- I find it difficult to navigate web sites that do not have provisions for error recovery.

Table 4.55. Table to Assess Response on Question 17B

Ques16B

		Frequency	Percent	Valid Percent	Cumulative Percent
Valid	Strongly Disagree	4	3.3	3.4	3.4
	Disagree	14	11.6	11.8	15.1
	Neutral	41	33.9	34.5	49.6
	Agree	48	39.7	40.3	89.9
	Strongly Agree	12	9.9	10.1	100.0
	Total	119	98.3	100.0	
Missing	System	2	1.7		
Total		121	100.0		

Q 17B -I prefer web sites where audio items are accompanied by (corresponding) text alternatives.

Table 4.56. Table to Assess Response on Question 17B

Ques17B

		Frequency	Percent	Valid Percent	Cumulative Percent
Valid	Strongly Disagree	4	3.3	3.3	3.3
	Disagree	18	14.9	14.9	18.2
	Neutral	57	47.1	47.1	65.3
	Agree	34	28.1	28.1	93.4
	Strongly Agree	8	6.6	6.6	100.0
	Total	121	100.0	100.0	

Q 18B-Background noise, echoes and reverberations from a website do not distract me when I am trying to listen to an online speech.

Table 4.57. Table to Assess Response on Question 18B

Ques18B

		Frequency	Percent	Valid Percent	Cumulative Percent
Valid	Strongly Disagree	12	9.9	9.9	9.9
	Disagree	47	38.8	38.8	48.8
	Neutral	32	26.4	26.4	75.2
	Agree	23	19.0	19.0	94.2
	Strongly Agree	7	5.8	5.8	100.0
	Total	121	100.0	100.0	

Q- 19B I have great difficulty in using the keyboard.

Table 4.58. Table to Assess Response on Question 19B

Ques19B

		Frequency	Percent	Valid Percent	Cumulative Percent
Valid	Strongly Disagree	72	59.5	60.0	60.0
	Disagree	37	30.6	30.8	90.8
	Neutral	2	1.7	1.7	92.5
	Agree	4	3.3	3.3	95.8

Table 4.58 —continued

		Frequency	Percent	Valid Percent	Cumulative Percent
	Strongly Agree	5	4.1	4.2	100.0
	Total	120	99.2	100.0	
Missing	System	1	.8		
Total		121	100.0		

Question 20 B: Users' portrayal of Computer Experience

Q-Do you think you have anything else to share with us about your computer/Internet experience?

Users were given an option to describe their general experience with computers (besides the ones they described within the bounds of two formatted questionnaires used for collecting data for the study), as their responses to question number twenty. Here are some excerpts from what they said:

In general people talked about their computer experiences in a negative manner. People reported that they "find the system confusing" and had "problems navigating the system." People also complained about having problems navigating the web due to lack of appropriate search terms.

People complained about their "lack of familiarity with computers" and even "found them intimidating due to lack of knowledge about how they work." General lack of familiarity with computers was so much that one respondent said his familiarity with the computer extended to knowing "how to turn it on." Also, people feared making mistakes and were scared of clicking or using the mouse on the apprehension that they "may make mistakes or wipe things off." On a higher level, people reported "having fears about learning new programs" or "loading new software."

135

On the positive side, people reported they are presently learning computers by "attending workshops" and "through self exploration." On the whole "the fear is ebbing and the computer experience is turning out to be a pretty enjoyable one," reports a self-identified "proficient" user.

The more comfortable users of computers, on the other hand, expressed their experience with computers with enthusiasm and gusto. They reported being "totally at ease" with the system, using it frequently as a "tool for communication with long lost friends and family," and for "buying merchandise like clothes shoes etc." Some reported that they "love cruising the web." One respondent reported that he even used the computer as a "tool for programming in dBase."

However, a couple of people reported that computers come with the inherent possibilities of "harming the eyes" because of the "small font size" and "not very clearly visible links"

A large majority of people refused to answer question number 20c.

Table 4.59. Validity and Reliability of the Scales

Component Matrix(a)

	Component	
	1	2
Ques1A	.770	
Ques2A	.892	
Ques3A		
Ques4A	.805	
Ques5A	.735	
Ques6A	.886	
Ques7A	.841	
Ques8A	-.815	
Ques9A	-.732	
Ques10A	-.737	

Table 4.59—continued

	Component	
	1	2
Ques11A		-.525
Ques12A	.750	
Ques13A	-.699	
Ques14A	.643	
Ques15A	-.614	

Extraction Method: Principal Component Analysis.
a. 2 components extracted.

A factor analysis was performed on the Modified
Computer Anxiety Scale (MCAS) questionnaire to unearth its
factor structure. Only two components with eigenvalues of
7.977 and 1.386 were retained. The variance explained by
the first component was 53.183% and the variance explained
by the second component was 9.243%. Together these
components explained 62.426% of the variances.

Questions 1A, 2A, 4A, 5A, 6A, 7A, 8A, 12A and 14A
contributed to the first component only, while questions
3A, 9A, 10A, 11A, and 13A contributed to the second
component only. Question 15A did not contribute to either
of the two principal components. However, the question was
not dropped from the questionnaire.

Component Analysis of the Scales of the Study

Table 4.60. Component Matrix(a)

	Component				
	1	2	3	4	5
Ques1B	.573				
Ques2B					
Ques3B	.609				
Ques4B					
Ques5B				.520	
Ques6B					
Ques7B			-.525		
Ques8B	.533	-.540			
Ques9B	.717				
Ques10B	.714				

Table 4.60 —continued

	Component				
	1	2	3	4	5
Ques11B		.591			
Ques12B	.554				
Ques13B		.604			
Ques14B		.515			
Ques15B			.619		
Ques16B	.636				
Ques17B					
Ques18B					.539
Ques19B	.590				

Extraction Method: Principal Component Analysis.
a. 5 components extracted.

A component analysis was performed on the 19 -item
Inherent Limitations of Systems and Web Design Scale
(ILSWS) for factor structure analysis. The first five
components had eigenvalues higher than one. The first
component had an eigenvalue 4.538 and explained 23.885% of
variance, the second component had an eigenvalue of 2.437
and explained 12.826% of variance, the third component had
an eigenvalue of 1.605 and explained 8.447% of the
variance, the fourth component had an eigenvalue of 1,450
and explained 7.634% of the variance, the fifth component
had an eigenvalue of 1.219 and explained 6.418% of the
variance. Together the first five components explained
59.209% of variance. Questions 1B, 3B, 8B, 9B, 10B, 12B,
16B & 19B contributed only to the first component.
Questions 11B, 13B, & 14B contributed only to the second
component. Questions 7B and 15B contributed to the third
component only. Question 5B contributed only the fourth
component, and question 18B contributed only to the fifth
component. Question 17B was found as not having contributed

138

to any component although it was retained as a
questionnaire item.

Since the scale is of an exploratory nature (designed
by the researcher for the present study), it was further
analyzed to determine whether it analyzed the same
constructs it was designed to measure; it was found out
that the questions associated with the first component
tended to measure mostly the visual and cognitive
constructs, the questions associated with the second
component tended to measure musculo-skeletal constructs,
questions 7B and 15B measured the cognitive and musculo-
skeletal constructs, while question 5B measured the visual
constructs, and question 18B measured the cognitive
construct (Stapleton, 1997).

Table 4.61. Reliability Statistics for MCAS

Cronbach's Alpha	Cronbach's Alpha Based on Standardized Items	N of Items
.927	.932	15

Table 4.62. Reliability Statistics for ILSWDS

Cronbach's Alpha	Cronbach's Alpha Based on Standardized Items	N of Items
.782	.770	19

The reliability measure used for the scales was
cronbach's alpha, the alpha coefficients were found to be
.927 (MCAS) and .782 (ILSWDS) for the two measures
respectively. Cronbach's alpha is frequently used by
researchers to establish the internal consistency construct

139

validity of scales. It goes to prove that there is at least a moderate correlation among the indicators of a concept and there is no need for more factors. The key idea here is to prove that different measures are measuring the same concept and thus they should be positively correlated with each other. Researchers opine that convergent validity and reliability merge as concepts when we tend to look at correlations among different measures of the same concept. The researcher's attempt to establish validity of the scale by convergent validity bore satisfactory results with a cronbach's alpha value of more than .60, considered well enough for exploratory purposes (Trochim, 2002).

CONCLUSION

The present study evaluated the impact of two major
variables which have been identified as creating barriers
to computer use and access among senior computer users: (i)
Age-related -infirmity (W/WT); (ii) *Computer-anxiety*.

The study was conducted on the main campus of Florida
State University. The subjects for the study were a sample
from among Florida State University's older adult teaching
and non-teaching permanent staff members. A set of three
questionnaires was administered to the selected individuals
to determine how the variables *age*, *gender* (M/F), *income*,
education, *computer-ownership* (O/NO), (computer) *experience,*
disability(D/ND) status etc., relate to the known barriers
of *age-related-infirmity(W/WT)* and *computer-anxiety*. The
study further investigated how the mentioned barrier
variables *age-related-infirmity (W/WT)* and *computer-anxiety*
in turn impede access to computer technology for senior
users.

Computer-anxiety is defined in the human computer
studies literature as a negative emotional or a negative
cognitive state experienced by users of computers when they
are actually using a computer or imagining future use of
it. Computer-anxiety has thus been termed as a state of
anxiety caused by a current situation, consisting of a
combination of affective (anxiety) and cognitive
(attitudinal) components. This means that anxiety produces
a tendency to cause worry, which decreases the ability of
the mind to concentrate on a task. Persons who have
experienced the trait of anxiety in certain situations may
transfer it to a similar situation. Studies suggest that
about a quarter to a third of computer users can be said to

141

be suffering from some kind of computer-related anxiety with a strong affective reaction towards using a computer (Chua, Chen & Wong, 1999; Cambre & Cook, 1985; Brosnan 1998; Eysenck & Calvo, 1992).

Research suggests that computer-anxious individuals manifest phobia-like symptoms which cause them to avoid using computers or make them reluctant to use computers. Internally, an anxious user lacks confidence in his/her ability to handle the technology and fears making mistakes. An anxious technophobe manifests unique anxiety symptoms like trembling, sweaty palms, heart palpitations, physical discomfiture, and a decreased level of psychological well being. Unlike a highly anxious user, an uncomfortable user also suffers from anxiety of more mild types. They often make negative statements about computers and are probably in need of more computer exposure to better appreciate the technology (Mahar, Henderson & Deane, 1997; Berntsen, 2005, Bozionelos 2001).

The existing literature identifies anxiety as a barrier, which decreases user performance (Desai & Richards, 1998; Mikulincer et al., 1990; Berntsen, 2005).

Much research has identified negative global attitudes towards computers as a prime factor in causing computer-anxiety. Studies conducted on computer users confirm that users who have more positive attitudes towards computers and have inherent trust in the technology show more interest in learning computers, which results in higher computer competence among them (Rosen & Weil, 1995; Korukonda, 2007; Ray, Sormunen, Harris, 2007).

142

Implications

Income, *Ownership* and (Computer) *Experience* – Significant
Variables Influencing *Computer Anxiety*

The current research confirmed some previous research
results. *Income*, *computer ownership* (*O/NO*) and the level of
experience with computers emerged as variables affecting
computer-anxiety for this population.

Experience (with computers) emerged as a powerful
underlying independent variable that tended to have a
strong inverse linear relation with the phenomenon of
computer-anxiety. Earlier research predicted the
possibilities that as a computer user's experience level
goes up there occurs a commensurate fall in his/her
computer-anxiety level (Wilfong, 2006; Yang, Mohamed, &
Beyerbach, 1999; Butchko, 2001, Havelka, Beasley, & Broome,
2004).

"Experience" (with computers), as a term has been
defined by researchers differently and so no single
definition emerges about what it means, although the
general convention is to quantify experience, in terms of
number of years of computer use or number of hours of usage
per week. Instead of quantifying experience (with
computers), some researchers discuss about the phenomenon
of experience in qualitative terms; they state that
students who had unpleasant prior experiences with
computers tended to be computerphobes, unlike the ones who
had positive prior experiences with computers(Doyle,
Stamouly & Haggard, 2005; Orr, 2007)

However, the most convincing explanation of (computer)
experience is linked to the concept of self-efficacy, which

143

means people's judgment of their abilities to organize and execute courses of action required to accomplish certain ends. It is not only the skill component itself, which is of crucial importance here, but it is also the belief that one's skill can be successfully employed to achieve computer-related experiences. Previous studies revealed the importance of experience in warding off computer-anxiety and confirm that people with previous experience with computers organize their work in more efficient ways compared to users with less experience. Thus, they conclude it is not simply the number of hours of computer-related-activity carried out by individuals which defines experience, but it is rather the users' skills in carrying out computer-related activities which count as an important criterion in defining experience. A typical disoriented user finds it hard to figure out the global structures of operating systems and the Internet and ends up accumulating negative experiences which leave him/her feeling much more disoriented (Compeau & Higgins, 1995; Shih, Munoz & Sanchez, 2006; Danielson, 2002; MCDonald &Stevenson, 1998; Schoon & Cafolla, 2002; Rada & Murphy, 1992; Otter & Johnson, 2000).

Besides (computer) experience, two other variables emerged as correlates of computer-anxiety in this study. They are individual's income and computer- ownership (O/NO) status.

Literature on the digital-divide testifies to the important role played by people's socio-economic status in determining access to computers and computer adaptation. Enders and Spas (2000) comment on the existing socio-economic schism in society and its consequent effect on

144

computer-ownership and computer usage in the following
manner:

> While the number of individuals with access to
> information tools is increasing, some Americans are
> being left behind. Minorities, low-income persons, the
> less-educated, and children of single-parent
> households, particularly those who live in rural areas
> and central cities, are among the groups that lack
> access to information resources.

Rubey (1999) constructed a comprehensive profile of
computer owners on the basis of factors like age, race,
education, income, region, etc. It was not surprising that
two out of the five variables influencing the factor of
computer-ownership were socio-economic in nature.

Leigh and Atkinson (2001) are of the opinion that some
of the sources of existing technological gaps in the
society can be taken care of by increased amount of income
accruing to households. According to statistics furnished
by the authors, an additional $10,000 accruing to the
households will make them 3.6 percentage points more likely
to own a computer and 2.0 percentage points more likely to
stay online. Thus we can see income plays an important role
in computer-ownership and adaptation to the technology of
computer. People in higher income groups are more likely to
own a computer and therefore less likely to be computer-
anxious.

Computer Anxiety **Emerged a Significant Predictor Variable for** *Barriers-to-Computer-Use*

Another major variable that was found to have a
significant relationship with its response variable

145

barriers-to-computer-use is *computer-anxiety*. The reason why *computer-anxiety* as a variable is of prime importance in this study is because it has been proven that older adult computer users suffer from comparatively higher levels of computer-anxiety (Laguna & Babcock, 1997; Igbaria & Parsuraman, 1989).

The literature review points out computer-anxiety as a significant barrier factor for older users that prevents them from fully exploiting the potentials offered by computer technology. The inhibitory effect of computer-anxiety was proven to have a stranglehold on users with higher levels of computer-anxiety, as it was found that these users reported higher rate of computer avoidance and lower levels of adjustment to computer technology. According to the Cognitive Interference Model of Computer Anxiety (CIM-CA), an anxious user goes through a cyclical process of self-doubt, disengagement, reconfrontation, renewed effort followed again by renewed doubt while interacting with computers (Smith & Caputi, 2007; Jackson et al, 2001; Barbiete & Weiss, 2004, Cody, Hoppin, & Wendt, 1999). This makes them suffer from an adverse effect on processing efficiency, so that many more of them report the prevalence of off-task and self-deprecatory thoughts when working with computers than their counterparts with less computer-anxiety. Besides, a number of studies have shown that computer-anxiety is a determinant of the amount of time a user spends online (Smith & Caputi, 2007; Jackson et al, 2001; Barbiete & Weiss, 2004, Cody, Hoppin, & Wendt, 1999).

Discussion

The current study failed to find any significant relationship between other fairly consistent correlates of the variable computer-anxiety such as age, gender (M/F), education, and disability (D/ND).

This is surprising as the over generalized conception about the nature of the relationship between the variables *age* and *computer-anxiety* is that a user's age is positively correlated (has a direct linear relationship) with the construct of computer-anxiety (Dyck & Smither, 1994; Igabaria & Parasuraman, 1989).A possible reason for this may be the narrow age range of the study's participants; only studies which include participants from a wide age range are known to report a significant relationship between the two variables (Chua, Chen, Wong, 1999).

Education level of users, which was thought to be inversely related with the variable *computer-anxiety* (Yang, Mohamed & Bayerbach, 1999; Henderson, Deane, Barrelle, & Mahar, 1995), was also found to have no relationship with computer-anxiety.

The variable *gender (M/F)* was also not found to be correlated with the variable *computer-anxiety*, unlike studies which conclusively reported differences in computer-anxiety levels based on *gender (M/F)*. In these studies women purportedly suffered from higher levels of computer-anxiety as compared to their male counterparts (Gilroy & Desai 1986; Dambrot et al., 1985; Rosen & Maguire 1990).

Much has been written in the digital divide literature about the negative relationship between the variables *computer-anxiety (O/NO)* and *disability (D/ND)*. This was of prime interest in the context of the present study, as a

147

majority of the elders are known to suffer from some level
of disability (Whitcomb, 2007, Kaye, 2000, Enders & Spas,
2000).

Contrary to expectations, the research failed to
establish a linear relationship between the variables *age*
and *age-related-infirmity (W/WT)*; this was deemed as an
interesting finding. This may be because of the fact that
the possible effect of the variable *age* on age-associated-
infirmities could not be properly vetted for this study.
The study's respondents belonging to various age categories
differed widely in numerical strengths, making comparisons
across categories a difficult proposition. While an
overwhelming number (110 or 90.9%) of the study's
respondents were from the age category 55-64, only 0.8% or
one respondent was from the age category 75 and above.
Also, since the population of the study represented a group
who are presently employed and hence highly functional,
chances are that the respondents of the present study are
in better shape physiologically, than their equivalent
counterparts who are not employed. Hence fewer respondents
reported infirmities related to old age.

Also, the research failed to prove any existing
relationship between the variables *age-related-infirmity*
(W/WT) and *barriers-to-computer-use*. The literature clearly
establishes that age-associated infirmities act as an
inhibitory factor for older users of computer technology,
by negatively affecting the performance of computer-related
tasks like clicking, pointing, etc. In a bid to overcome
this barrier, the literature calls for the establishment of
senior-centered interface-design -guidelines to accommodate
elderly users suffering from age-related-infirmities

148

(Zajicek, 2007; Czaja, 2007; Kurniawan & Zaphiris, 2007;
Worden & Walker, 2007).

The present study, however, was successful in
endorsing the validity of the established factors which
spur or thwart the older users in general, to take to
increased computer use or alternatively decrease such uses.

Based on the results of the study, a new and valid
model emerged that only highlights the significant
relationships between the variables involved in the
research:

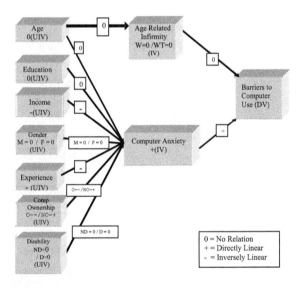

**Figure 13. A model representing the actual relationship among the
variables of the study (Designed by Bonny Bhattacharjee).**

```
How to interpret a dichotomous relationship:
Example: Computer Ownership (O=-/NO=+) =A person who owns a computer is less likely to
suffer from computer anxiety (represented by a - sign signifying an inverse
relationship with the variable Computer Anxiety) compared to his /her counterpart who
does not own a computer.
```

Key:
```
       UIV- Underlying independent variable
       IV- Independent Variable
       DV- Dependent Variable
```

The Variables Found to be Significant and the Trends in the Literature

The variables which were found to have some kind of relationship with the variable *computer-anxiety* are: (Computer) *Experience*, *Income* and *Computer Ownership* (*O/NO*).

The Variable (Computer) *Experience*: Most studies on computer-anxiety suggest that the phenomenon is negatively correlated (shares an inverse linear relationship) with the variable (computer) *experience*. It is emphasized that as users gain experience with computers, their computer-anxiety is reduced. The present study also endorses this viewpoint (Koohang, 1989; Liu, Reed, & Phillips, 1992; Savenye, Davidson, & Orr, 1992; Reed & Overbaugh, 1993; Maurer & Simonson, 1993-1994; Rosen & Weil, 1994; Necessary & Parish, 1996).

The Variable *Income*: Research reveals that people with higher incomes are less likely to suffer from computer-anxiety. This is because higher incomes makes ownership of computers a possibility which in turn guarantees the users in higher income brackets greater exposure to computer technology, thereby helping to counter techno-phobic tendencies among them. The most computer-anxious users are identified as hailing from lower socio-economic classes with very little exposure to computers. Studies confirm

that people hailing from households having higher levels of
income tend to be more computer-savvy and exhibit greater
tendencies to use computers at work places (Simon, 1996;
Lippincott & Wilkins, 2003). It can thus be concluded that
the variable *income* is negatively correlated (shares an
inverse linear relationship) with the variable *computer-
anxiety*. The study's result upholds this viewpoint.
The Variable *Computer Ownership* (*O/NO*): A review of the
literature reveals that people with higher levels of
exposure to computer technology are more likely to own
computers. Thus, it may be hypothesized that greater
exposure to the technology of computer, predisposes people
to own a computer by significantly reducing fear and
apprehension among users with respect to usage of computer
technology. Thus literature has identified computer-anxiety
as a significant factor leading to computer non-ownership
(Laffey & Musser, 1998).It can be stated then that the
dichotomous variable *computer-ownership* (*O/NO*) has a two-
fold relationship with the variable *computer-anxiety* with
computer-ownership (*O*) sharing a direct linear relationship
with the variable *computer-anxiety*, and *computer ownership*
(*NO*)- sharing a negative relationship with the variable
computer-anxiety. This means people who own computers tend
to suffer from less computer-anxiety as opposed to their
equivalent counterparts who do not own computers. The
results of the present study also support this viewpoint.
**The Literature Review and Other Variables and the Study's
Conclusion**
The Variable *Age*- The present study failed to establish any
correlation between the demographic variables *age* and
computer-anxiety. Although, some authors conclude that the
variable *age* is positively correlated (shares a direct

linear relationship) with the variable *computer-anxiety*, a large number of studies reveal mixed results. From nine non-statistical reports reviewed for the purpose of proving conclusively the relationship between the variables *age* and *computer-anxiety*, only two revealed an age correlation, four revealed no age correlation, and the other three showed *age* as being correlated with some measures of the variable *computer-anxiety* (Rosen & Maguire, 1990;Dyck & Smither, 1994; Igabaria & Parasuraman, 1989).

The Variable *Gender*: The present study failed to establish any correlation between the variables *gender (M/F)* and *computer-anxiety*. The literature, however, succeeds in establishing a correlation between the variables *gender (M/F)* and *computer-anxiety*. Rosen and Maguire (1990) reviewed 25 studies and concluded that females suffer from higher levels of computer-anxiety than their equivalent male counterparts.

The variable *Education:* Torkzadeh and Angulo (1992) point out that education is found to be an antidote to computer-anxiety that aids the process of comfortable computer usage and better realization of computing potentials. The authors are of the opinion that education and training of end users in acquiring skills towards system utilization can help ward off some fear and feelings of apprehension associated with computer technology usage. Research also proves that education fosters greater computer confidence in users, leading to reduction of computer-anxiety among them. Also users with more education tend to manifest greater degrees of interest and knowledge in computing, which tend to combat the strains of computer-phobia among them (Ellis & Allaire, 1999; Yang, Mohamed & Beyerbach, 1999). All in all, the literature review points towards an inverse linear

152

(or positive) association between the variables *education* and *computer-anxiety*. However, the present research fails to uphold any such viewpoints.

The Variable *Disability*- It is known that the variable *disability (D/ND)* inhibit computer use among the disabled by reducing access. It is but a common knowledge that people with disabilities have reduced access to computers and the Internet. As stated earlier, only about 24% of Americans with disabilities own a computer as compared to about 52% of their non-disabled counterparts, while only 11% of people with disabilities have Internet access as compared to 31% of their counterparts who are not disabled. Thus, *disability (W/WT)* as a variable is assumed to have a direct linear relationship with the variable *computer-anxiety*-the latter stemming from decreased exposure to computers ("Access to Computers," 2006; "Specific Barriers to Web Access," 1999; "Disability and the Digital Divide," 2007). The present study, however, failed to find any significant relationship between the variables *disability (W/WT)* and *computer-anxiety*.

The Independent Variables: Their Significance

A significant accomplishment of the study lay in establishing the fact that *computer-anxiety* as a variable has a direct linear relationship with the dependent variable of the study *barriers-to-computer-use*, an idea that finds overwhelming support in the existing computer--anxiety literature, which dubs computer-anxiety as a barrier factor in technology access. Thus, it is widely presumed that a rise in computer-anxiety is accompanied by increasing difficulty in accessing computers (Torkzadeh &

Angulo, 1992; Benson, 2001; Doyle, Stamouli & Huggard, 2005; Rosen & Maguire, 1990).

The other independent variable of the study *age-related-infirmity (W/WT)* was found to have a no correlation with the dependent variable of the study, *barriers-to-computer-use*, although literature review revealed that *age-related-infirmity (W)* tend to thwart users' ability to access computers (Zajicek, 2007; Czaja, 2007; Kurniawan & Zaphiris, 2007).

Thus, we can conclude that despite all its limitations the present study was largely successful in confirming the trend established in the literature review.

Limitations of the study

The study has its limitations, as the study was conducted within the backdrop of Florida State University's Tallahassee campus; hence, the study's results are not generalizable to the overall older computer user population.

Some important variables which find mention in traditional computer-anxiety literature were left out of the study due to parsimony. One of these variables is *math-anxiety* (a learned fearful emotional response to participating in mathematics classes), which is known to have a significant effect on the phenomenon of computer-anxiety and is proven to be a good predictor of anxiety towards computers (Howard & Smith, 1986; Morrow, Prell, & McElroy, 1986; Baker, 1985; Russell et al., 2007).

The omission of the variable *math-anxiety*, is particularly noteworthy as researchers identify it as one of the consistent correlates of the variable *computer-anxiety* along with gender, age, (computer) experience, etc. Howard (1986), Igbaria and Parasuraman (1989), Morrow et

154

al. (1986), and Raub (1981) reported math-anxiety as a significant factor, inducing computer-anxiety. Rosen and Maguire (1990) reported results from 10 research reports which found that mathematics-anxiety and computer-anxiety were positively correlated.

The *college-of-enrollment* (academic major) could have been another potentially important variable for the present study, especially because the study was executed in the backdrop of an institution of higher education.

Havelka, Beasley, & Broome (2004) conducted a study among 331 undergraduate business students. The researchers wanted to determine among other things whether there are differences in levels of computer-anxiety among the students belonging to various business disciplines. In general, the results supported the premise that there are differences in computer-anxiety levels among the various business disciplines, with MIS majors showing the lowest amount of computer-anxiety. The difference was explained with the idea that students with MIS as their major experience a greater intensity of interaction with computers as they have to do a majority of their assignments using computers.

Studies with *academic majors* as predictor variables were also conducted by other researchers, as well. Their importance lay in determining exactly what disciplines or academic areas have a greater prevalence of higher computer-anxiety so that actions could be taken to bring it down among people who would benefit from them most (Bowers et al.; 1996, Burkett et al. 2001).

Although, these studies were conducted with a younger population the results are indicative of trends that may be established early in life.

155

Suggestions for Future Research

It is suggested that any future researchers replicate the results of the study in varying backdrops so as to help academia arrive at a more generalizable conclusion regarding the relationships between the study's variables.

APPENDIX A

A.1 The Scale Names, Scale Description and Studies
identified by their Author(s).

Author/s of the Study	Scale Name	Scale Description
Anthony, Clarke,& Anderson (2000)	1.MTI(Rosen & Weil; 1992)	1. MTI (Rosen &Weil; 1992) CARS-C CTS-C *GATC-C – * presents 20 statements of attitudes towards using computers and related technology (Anthony, Clarke & Anderson, 2000)
	2.NEO-FFI (Form S)(Revised NEO-PI-R by Costa Jr. & McCrae;1985)	2. The NEO-PI-R is a psychological personality inventory with 240 questions (Anthony, Clarke,& Anderson, 2000).
Mcilroy et al.(2007) & McIlroy et al. (2001)	1. CARS (Rosen & Weil; 1992).	1. A 20-item 5 -point Likert-type scale for measuring an individual's computer anxiety level (Mcilroy et al., 2007; McIlroy et al, 2001).

	2. CTS (Rosen &Weil; 1992).	2. A 20-item scale with a 5-point Likert-type format (ranging from 1="not at all", through to 5="very often." With 11 items phrased in the negative direction and 9 items in the positive direction. Respondents are asked how often their thoughts are in accord with each statement (Mcilroy et al., 2007; McIlroy et al, 2001).
Laguna & Babcock (1997)	CAIN (Montag, Simonson & Maurer;1984).	A standardized instrument for measuring a feeling of anxiety towards computer, containing twenty-six positively or negatively worded Likert-type items (Yu,DiGangi, Jannasch - Pennell & Collins, 2007).

Ellis & Allaire (1999)	Raub Scale (Raub; 1982).	A 10-item 5-point Likert-type scale used for gauging a subject's computer anxiety level (Ellis & Allaire, 1999).
Butchko (2003)	CAS (Marcoulides; 1989).	A 20 item Likert-type computer-anxiety scale, with five options, ranging from 1 -not at all to 5 -very much (Frideris, Goldenberg, & Fleising, 2006).
Brosnan (1999)	CARS (Heinssen, Glass & Knight; 1987).	A 19-item scale used for gauging an individual's computer anxiety level; with 5 options from 1 (Strongly Disagree) to 5 (Strongly Agree) for registering responses (Hopson, 2001).
Durndell & Haag (2002).	1. CARS (Heinssen, Glass & Knight; 1987).	1. A 19-item scale for measuring individuals' computer anxiety level(Hopson,

		2001).
	2. IAS (A modified CAS by Nickell & Pinto; 1986).	2.A scale used for gauging individuals' attitude towards the Internet (Durndell & Haag, 2002).
	3. CSE (Torkzadeh & Koufteros,1994).	3. A scale used for measuring an individual's belief about his/her ability to perform a computer-related task. It is a 5-point Likert-type scale, ranging from 1 meaning "very little confidence" to 5 signifying a "lot of confidence" (Decker, 1998).
Sam,Othman, & Nordin (2005)	1.CARS (Heinssen, Glass & Knight; 1987).	1.A 19-item scale for measuring individuals' computer anxiety level(Hopson, 2001).

	2. CSE (Torkzadeh & Koufteros, 1994; Murphy, Coover, & Owen, 1989).	2.A 29-item, five-point Likert type scale (1=strongly disagree through to 5=strongly agree) used for gauging a subjects' ability to use computers. Each item begins with the phrase "I feel confident" (Sam, Othamn, & Nordin, 2005).
Bozionelos (2004)	CARS (Rosen & Weil; 1992).	A Likert-type scale for measuring an individual's computer anxiety level (Bozionelos, 2004).
McInerney, McInerney & Sinclair (1990).	CARS (Rosen, Sears &Weil, 1987).	A scale that measures anxiety about present or future interactions with computers or computer-related technology (McInerney, McInerney & Sinclair, 1990).
Yang, Mohamed & Beyerbach (1999)	Short form of COMPAS (Oetting, 1983).	A scale used for measuring an individual's

		level of computer anxiety. The short form of the COMPAS consists of Likert-type items for which respondents report their subjective feelings of anxiety (Yang, Mohamed & Beyerbach, 1999).

APPENDIX B

Survey: Use of Computers By Older Adults (age 55 years and above): For Determining How the Access Factors Affect the Constraining Influences in Computer/Internet Use.

B.1 Section A: Computer Anxiety

The following statements refer to your experiences with computers. Read each of the following statements and respond according to how you generally feel about the idea expressed in the item.

		Strongly Agree	Agree	Neutral	Disagree	Strongly Disagree
1	I feel anxious whenever I am using computers.					
2.	I am nervous when I sit down at the computer.					
3.	I am confident in my ability to use computers.					
4.	I feel tense whenever working on a computer.					
5.	I worry about making mistakes on the computer.					
6.	I try to avoid using					

	computers whenever possible.					
7.	I experience anxiety whenever I sit in front of a computer terminal.					
8.	I enjoy working with computers.					
9.	I would like to continue working with computers in the future.					
10.	I feel relaxed when I am working on a computer.					
11.	I wish that computers were not as important as they are.					
12.	Computers frighten me.					
13.	I feel content when I am working on a computer.					

14.	I feel overwhelmed when I am working on a computer.					
15.	I feel at ease with computers.					

C.1 Section B: Inherent Limitations of Systems and Web Design

The following statements refer to your experiences with computers/Internet. Read each of the following statements and respond according to how you generally feel about the idea expressed in the item.

		Strongly Agree	Agree	Neutral	Disagree	Strongly Disagree
1.	I have difficulty reading a text size smaller than 14-point on the screen.					
2.	I prefer computer texts that are neither very big nor very small.					
3.	I have difficulty reading computer texts that appear too crowded.					
4.	I prefer online texts, which appear in clearly identifia					

	ble sections.				
5.	I prefer contrast in colors between the backgroun d and the text displayed on the screen.				
6.	I do not prefer patterned backgroun ds.				
7.	I think animated Graphics and videos should always be accompani ed by text.				
8.	I have difficult y dealing with features like blinking texts.				
9.	I have difficult y moving through web sites, which have				

	automatic ally scrolling texts.				
10.	I have difficult y navigatin g a site, which does not have labeled (hyper) links.				
11.	I prefer web sites that have site maps.				
12.	I prefer web sites that have clearly visible buttons and icons.				
13.	I prefer pull down menus, which appears when I select an item with a mouse.				
14.	I prefer websites that are just a mouse click away.				
15.	I do not prefer web				

	sites, which require extensive scrolling .					
16.	I find it difficult to navigate web sites that do not have provisions for error recovery.					
17.	I prefer web sites where audio items are accompanied by (corresponding) text alternatives.					
18.	Background noise, echoes and reverberations from a website do not distract me when I am trying to listen to an online speech.					
19.	I have					

	great difficulty in using the keyboard.					

20. Do you think you have anything else to share with us about your computer/Internet experience?

APPENDIX D

D.1 Section C: Demographic Questionnaire

Please feel free to provide your responses to the following questions, and tick (\/) each mentioned response, for a question, against appropriate category:

1. Your age (In years):

Under 55 ------------------
55-64   --------------------
65-74 ---------------------
75 and Above----------------

2.Your gender status: Male ----------------------- **Female-**

3.Your income (To the nearest thousand dollars):

Under 30,000 -------------------
30, 000-40,000 ------------------
40,000-50,000-------------------
50,000-60,000-------------------
60,000 and Above----------------

4.The most recent degree you have attained (No certificates or diplomas, please):

High School -----------------
Associate -------------------
Bachelors--------------------
Master's---------------------
Specialist-------------------
Ph.D.------------------------

5. Do you have a personal computer at home? Yes -----------
------**No**---------------------

6. Years of computing experience you have (To the nearest whole number, in year/s)? :

Below ½ year
½ year -1 year

171

1year- 2 years
2-years -3 years
3 years - 4years
4 years -5 years
5 years and Above

7. **Do you suffer from any disability/disabilities? (Yes)** -----
-------- **(No)** -------------

8. **Very briefly state the disability/disabilities you
suffer from (Please ignore this question if you have marked
"No" to question # 7):** -----------------------------------
--

9.**Is it /are these disability/disabilities congenital (from
birth)? (Answer this question only if you have answered
question # 8): (Yes)** -----------------------

(No) ---
-----

10. **At what age (state in numbers) did the
disability/disabilities set in? (Please ignore this
question if you have marked "Yes" to question #9):** --------
----

11. **Do you think this (disability/disabilities) is/are a
part of the general process of aging (arising from such
age-related incidents as arthritis, cancer, stroke etc.)?
(Please answer this question only if you have answered
question # 10): (Yes)** --------------------- **(No)** -----------

12. **What is your job designation?   Faculty** --------
Staff -----------

13. **The people you work with are primarily involved with
(circle one): Humanities** ------- **Social Sciences** ---------
---- **Science+ Tech** ---------------------- **Other** ---------
--------- **(Administration, Professional, Support Staff etc)**

APPENDIX E

E.1 FSU Human Subjects Committee Approval Letter

Office of the Vice President For Research
Human Subjects Committee
Tallahassee, Florida 32306-2742
(850) 644-8673 . FAX (850) 644-4392

APPROVAL MEMORANDUM

Date: 2/21/2007

To: Bonny Bhattacharjee

Address: 1 Palmeto Drive, # 422, Tallahassee, Fl-32304-
8098, P.O. Box-62180
Dept.: COLLEGE OF INFORMATION

From: Thomas L. Jacobson, Chair

Re: Use of Human Subjects in Research
Factors Affecting Computer Use Among Older Adult Users: A
Study in the Backdrop of Florida State University

The forms that you submitted to this office in regard to
the use of human subjects in the proposal referenced above
have been reviewed by the Secretary, the Chair, and two
members of the Human Subjects Committee. Your project is
determined to be Expedited per 45 CFR § 46.110(7) and has
been approved by an expedited review process.

The Human Subjects Committee has not evaluated your
proposal for scientific merit, except to weigh the risk to
the human participants and the aspects of the proposal
related to potential risk and benefit. This approval does
not replace any departmental or other approvals, which may
be required.

If you submitted a proposed consent form with your
application, the approved stamped consent form is attached
to this approval notice. Only the stamped version of the
consent form may be used in recruiting research subjects.

If the project has not been completed by 2/20/2008 you must
request a renewal of approval for continuation of the

173

project. As a courtesy, a renewal notice will be sent to you prior to your expiration date; however, it is your responsibility as the Principal Investigator to timely request renewal of your approval from the Committee.

You are advised that any change in protocol for this project must be reviewed and approved by the Committee prior to implementation of the proposed change in the protocol. A protocol change/amendment form is required to be submitted for approval by the Committee. In addition, federal regulations require that the Principal Investigator promptly report, in writing any unanticipated problems or adverse events involving risks to research subjects or others.

By copy of this memorandum, the Chair of your department and/or your major professor is reminded that he/she is responsible for being informed concerning research projects involving human subjects in the department, and should review protocols as often as needed to insure that the project is being conducted in compliance with our institution and with DHHS regulations.

This institution has an Assurance on file with the Office for Human Research Protection. The Assurance Number is IRB00000446.

Cc: Dr. Corinne Jorgensen, Advisor
HSC No. 2007.285

F.1 Sample Informed Consent Letter

Factors Affecting Computer Use Among Older Adult Users: A Study in the Backdrop of Florida State University

This is to let you know that Bonny Bhattacharjee, currently researching under Professor Dr. Corinne Jorgensen, of College of Information, and a graduate student of Florida State University, has requested my participation in a research study, to be executed at Florida State University's (Tallahassee campus) premises.

The purpose of the research is to determine how the various factors in information technology usage, like income, education, age, ownership of PCs etc., interact with users' perceptions about computers and finally the phenomenon of computer usage among them . The significance of the study lies in the fact that this is a study on older adult (age 55 years or above) end users, who may face severe limitations, from both physical and socio-economic perspectives, when it comes to the issue of interacting with information technologies like computer and the Internet. Previous studies, conducted on average older adults, have reported such limitations, that the population faces. The uniqueness of the study is that it is being conducted to determine whether relatively well-off older adults, in terms of socio-economic and skill related indicators like education, income, years of experience etc., also face similar constraints with the mentioned information technologies, like their average counterparts. The potential subjects of the study will be from among Florida State University's older adult (55 years of age or older) teaching and non-teaching permanent staff members. The subjects will be selected randomly by the process of stratified random sampling. I understand that (if I qualify as a subject) my participation will involve filling out a three-part questionnaire. I also understand that if I do not qualify as a subject (in terms of required age or employment status) of the study, I would have to withdraw from the study by not filling out the three-part questionnaire. The questionnaires will contain a total of forty-nine questions (forty-five questions for those without any disabilities forty-seven questions for people with congenital disabilities and forty-nine questions for people with age-related-infirmities), requiring "yes"/"no" answers, check marks against appropriate categories from respondents, or requiring respondents to use words to state their disabilities, the age (of the respondent) at which the disability set in, etc. For most part respondents would have to register their responses on likert-type scales. Only one non-mandatory question (in the second questionnaire), would require the respondents to state fully in words their opinions/experiences about computer/Internet usages, along lines different from the ones suggested in the questionnaire.

I understand that it will take me about twenty minutes to fill out the first and second part of the questionnaire, and about ten minutes to fill out the third part of the questionnaire. This is, however, estimation, and in reality, the time for completing each part of the questionnaire may be a trifle more or less. However, I can take up to five to seven (5-7) days to return the completed questionnaire to the researcher or her assistant, when he/she (re)visits me to collect the completed questionnaires. Participation in this study will not entitle me to any direct benefits; also I see no foreseeable risk or the possibility of discomfort if I participate in this study.

The results of this study will be published, but the identity of subjects like me will not be revealed. Instead of identifying my responses against my name, the researcher would identify my responses against a code assigned to the questionnaire I have filled out. Also my name would not be sought in the first place, as it has no significance for the research design.

I am aware that the data of the study which will come in text format shall be preserved for a period of three years in a locked file cabinet, inside a large envelope, at the doctoral study room at the College of Information, after which it shall be destroyed.

I understand that I won't be paid for my participation in this study, however, any question I may have about this study, before and after my consent, can be directed to:

Bonny Bhattacharjee at the e-mail address bb02e@garnet.acns.fsu.edu, or to my   supervisor/chair Professor Dr. Corinne Jorgensen @ cjorgensen@ci.fsu.edu

The nature, demands, benefits, and the potential of risks of the study, have been explained to me, and I consent to participate with full knowledge of each. Although, I do not see any potential risk for participation in this study, if I have any questions about my rights, as a participant in this research, or if I feel, even remotely, that I have been placed at risk, I can contact the Chair of the Human Subjects Committee, Institutional Review Board, through the Office of the Vice President for Research, at (850) 644-8633.

I affirm a copy of this consent form was given to me, and after having read the consent form, I clearly comprehend that I may withdraw my consent and discontinue participation at any time without penalty or loss of benefits to which I may otherwise be entitled. I also understand that in reviewing and returning this consent form I have consented to participate in the present study, however, by doing so I am not waiving any legal claims, rights or remedies.

REFERENCES

Access North. (2007). *Disability and digital divide.*
Retrieved October 19, 2006, from
http://accessnorth.net/legis/disstats.html

Adler, R.P. (1995). Older adults and computers: Report of a
national survey. Tech Report, San Francisco: Senior Net.

Agelight LLC. (2004). *Interface design guidelines for users
of all ages.* Retrieved from
http://www.agelight.com/webdocs/designguide.pdf

Algharibi, M. (n.d.). *Computer and Internet World.*
Retrieved March 3, 2005, from
http://www.mazoon.8m.com/computer.htm

American Statistical Association.(2007).*What is a survey?*
(n.d.). Retrieved September 02, 2005, from
http://www.amstat.org/sections/srms/brochures/survwhat.html

Anderson, J.E.(1999). *Simple Random Sampling.* Retrieved
July 24, 2006, from
http://cda.mrs.umn.edu/~anderson/math1601/notes/ch3/node6.h
tml

Anderson, J. (2005). *Over-55 Users - A Gray Area for
Internet Growth.* Retrieved August 3, 2006, from
http://www.ergoweb.com/news/detail.cfm?id=1104

Anthony, L.M., Clarke, M.C., & Anderson, S.J. (2000).
Technophobia and personality subtypes in a sample of South
African university students. *Computers in Human Behavior,
16*(1).Retrieved May 28, 2007, from PsychInfo database.

Archambault, S.(2000).*One-way ANOVA* from Psychology
Department at the Wellesley College Website:
http://www.wellesley.edu/Psychology/Psych205/indepttest.htm
l

Avoleo, B.J., Walsman, D.A., & McDANIEL, M.A. (1990). Age
and work performance in nonmanagerial jobs: The effects of
experience and occupational type. *Academy of Management
Journal, 33,* 407-422.

178

Baker, J. E. (1985). Attitudes of Maine cooperative extension service personnel towards computerization. *Research in Rural Education, 2* (4), 159-162.

Baldi, R.A. (1997).Training older adults to use the computer issues related to the workplace, attitudes and training. *Educational Gerontology, 23*, 453-465.

Barbiete, F., Weiss, E.(2004). Computer self efficacy and anxiety scales for an Internet sample: Testing measurement equivalence of existing measures and development of new scales. *Computers in Human Behavior, 20*, 1-15.

Bartel, A.P., & Sicherman, N. (1993). Technological Change and retirement decisions of older workers. *Journal of Labor Economics, 11*, 162-183.

Benson, S.J.(2001). *Computer anxiety: Impediment to Technology integration?* Retrieved August 27, 2006, from http://pt3.nmsu.edu/educ621/sharon2.html

Bernard, M., Liao, C., & Mills, M. (2001). Determining the best online font for older adults. *Usability News, 3.1.*

Berntsen, J. (2005). *Computer anxiety.* Retrieved May 9, 2007, from http://coe.sdsu.edu/eet/articles/computeranxiety/index.htm

Bethea, L.S. (2002). *Older adult barriers to the internet: An intergenerational approach to usability and health outcomes.* Retrieved July 19, 2005, from http://apha.confex.com/apha/130am/techprogram/paper_51375.htm

Bhattacharjee, B. (2006). *Inherent Limitations of Systems and Web Design Scale.* Tallahassee, Fl: Florida State University.

Bhattacharjee, B. (2006). *Modified Computer Anxiety Scale.* Tallahassee, Fl: Florida State University.

Bikson, T., & Panis, C.(1995). *Citizens, computers, and connectivity: A review of trends.* Retrieved May 26, 2006, from http://www.rand.org.

Borghans, L., & Weel, B. (2002). *Do older workers have more trouble using a computer than younger workers?* Retrieved

May 27, 2006, from http://edata.ub.unimaas.nl/www-edocs/loader/file.asp?id=581

Bowers, D.A.J. & V.M. Bowers. (1996). Assessing and coping with computer anxiety in the social science classroom. *Social Science Review*, *14*(4), 439-443. Bozinelos, N.(2001). Computer anxiety: Relationship with computer experience and prevalence. *Computers in Human Behavior*, *17*, 213-214.

Bozinelos, N. (2004). Socio-economic background and computer use: the role of computer anxiety and computer experience in their relationship. *International Journal of Human-Computer Studies*, *61* (5), 725-746.

Brosnan, M. J. (1998). The impact of psychological gender, gender-related perceptions, significant others, and the introducer of technology upon computer anxiety in students. *Journal of Educational Computing Research*, *18*, 63-78.

Brosnan, M.J. (1999).The impact of and self-efficacy upon performance. *Journal of Computer Assisted Learning*, *14* (3), 223-234.

Burkett, W.H., D.M. Compton, & G.G. Burkett. (2001). An examination of computer attitudes, anxieties, and aversions among diverse college populations: Issues central to understanding information sciences in the new millennium. *Informing Science*, *4*(3), 77-85.

Butchko, L.A. (2000).*Computer Experience and anxiety:Older versus younger workers*. Retrieved May 20, 2006 from http://www.iusb.edu/~journal/2001/butchko.html

Cambre, M.A., & Cook, D.L.(1985). *Computer anxiety*: Definition, measurement and correlates. *Journal of Educational Computing Research*, *1* (1), 37-54.

Carpenter, M. (n.d.). *Older wiser wired: Working to bridge the digital divide*. Retrieved May 27, 2006, from http://www.aarp.org/olderwiserwired/oww-features/Articles/a2003-11-19-ia-perspectives.html

Cassidy, S., & Eachus, P.(n.d.).[Home page]. Retrieved January 28, 2007 from http://www.chssc.salford.ac.uk/healthSci/selfeff/SELFEFFa.htm

Charness, N. (Ed.) (1985). *Aging and human performance.*
Chichester, UK: John Wiley & Sons.

Charness, N., Bosman, E., & Elliot, R.G. (1995). *Senior-friendly input devices: Is the pen mightier than the mouse?*
Retrieved April 19, 2000, from
http://www.psy.fsu.edu/~charness/apa95/

Charness, N. & Holley, P. (2004). The New Media and Older
Adults: Usable and Useful? *American Behavioral Scientist,*
48, 416-433.

Charness, N.H., Kelley, C.L., & Bosman, E.A, & Mottram,
M.(2001).Training and retraining of novice and experienced
adults in word processing: Effects of age and interface.
Psychology and Aging, 16, 110-127.

Chua, S., Chen, D. & Wong, A.F.L. (1999). Computer anxiety
and its correlates: A meta-analysis. *Computers in Human
Behavior, 15,* 609-623.

Cochran, W.G.(1977).*Sampling techniques* (3rd ed.). John
Wiley :New York.

Cody, M., Hoppin, S., & Wendt, P.(1999).Silver surfers:
Training and evaluating internet use among older adult
learners. *Communication Education, 48* (4), 269-286.

Comber, C., Colley, A., Hargreaves, D. J., Dorn, L. (1997).
The effects of age, gender, and computer experience upon
computer attitudes. *Educational Research, 39,* 123-133.

Compeau, D. R. and C. Higgins (1995). Computer self-
efficacy: Development of a measure and initial test. *MIS
Quarterly, 19*(2), 189-211.

Costa, P.T. Jr., & McCrae R. R. (1985). *The NEO Personality
Inventory Manual.* Odessa, FL: Psychological Assessment
Resources.

Cohen, B.A., & Waugh, G.W. (1989). Assessing computer
anxiety. *Psychological Reports, 65,* 735-738.

Cooley, S., Deitch, I., Harper, M., Hinrichsen, G., Lopez,
M., & Molinari, V. (1997). *What practitioners should know*

about working with older adults. Retrieved May 29, 2006 from http://www.apa.org/pi/aging/practitioners.pdf

Czaja, S. J. (1996).Aging and acquisition of Computer Skills. In W. A. Rodgers, A. D. Fisk & N. Walker (Eds.), *Aging and Skilled Performance: Advances in Theory and Applications*,(pp.201-221). New Jersey: Lawrence Erlbaum Associates, Inc.

Czaja, S. J. (1997). The Role of Human Factors Engineering in Systems Design and Evaluation. In G. Salvendy (Ed.),*The Handbook of Human Factors and Ergonomics* (2nd Ed.).United States: John Wiley and Sons.

Czaja, S.(2003).[Home Page]. Retrieved May 27, 2006, from http://www.med.miami.edu/psychiatry/create.html

Czaja, S.(n.d.).*The impact of aging on access to technology*. Retrieved May 20, 2007, from PsychInfo database.

Dambrot, F. H., Watkins-Malek, M. A., Silling, S. M. Marshall, R. S., & Garver, J. A. (1985). Correlates of sex differences in attitudes toward and involvement with computers. *Journal of Vocational Behavior*, *27*, 71-86.

Danielson, D. (2002). Web navigation and the behavioral effects of constantly visible site maps. *Interacting with Computers*, *14*, 611-618.

Davies, A.R., Klawe, M., Ng, M., Nyhus, C.,Sullivan, H.(n.d.). *Gender issues in computer science education*. Retrieved October 30, 2005, from http://www.wcer.wisc.edu/archive/nise/News Activities/Forums/Klawepaper.htm

Decker, C. A.(1998). Perceptions of computer use self-efficacy among university employees. *Journal of Vocational and Technical Education*,*14* (2). Retrieved July 1, 2007, from http://209.85.165.104/search?q=cache:kvsIGSUZefwJ:scholar.l ib.vt.edu/ejournals/JVTE/v14n2/JVTE-3.html+CSE+(Torkzadeh+%26+Koufteros,1994%3B+Training+transf er+perception+of+computer+use+self+efficacy+among+universit y+employees,+CArol+A+decker&hl=en&ct=clnk&cd=1&gl=us

Department of Elder Affairs.(2005).*Elder affairs and agency for workforce innovation praise older workers.* Retrieved April 22, 2006, from http://elderaffairs.state.fl.us/News/PressReleases/2005/Jul -Sep/092205.html

Desai, M.S., & T.C., Richards.(1998). Computer Anxiety, Training and Education: A Meta Analysis. *Journal of Information Systems Education, 9*(1 & 2), 49-54.

Doyle, E., Stamouli, I., & Huggard, M. (2005). *Computer anxiety, self efficacy, computer experience: An investigation throughout a computer science degree.* Retrieved August 20, 2007, from http://fie.engrng.pitt.edu/fie2005/papers/1693.pdf

Durndell, A., & Haag, Z.(2002).Computer Self-Efficacy, Computer Anxiety, Attitudes Toward the Internet and Reported Experience with the Internet, by Gender, in an East European Sample. *Computers in Human Behavior 18*, 521-535.

Dutta, R.(1992).The relationship between flexibility-rigidity and the primary mental abilities. Unpublished doctoral dissertation, Pennsylvania State University.

Dyck, J.L., & Smither, J. A.(1994). Age differences in computer anxiety: The role of computer experience, gender and education. *Journal of Educational Computing Research, 10*, 239-248.

Echt, K.V. (2002). Designing web-based health information for older adults: Visual considerations and design directives. In R.W. Morrell (Ed.), *Older adults, health information, and the World Wide Web,* (pp. 61-87). Mahwah, New Jersey: Erlbaum.

Echt, K.V., Morrell, R.W., Park, D.C.(1998). The effects of age and training formats on basic computer skill acquisition in older adults. *Educational Gerontology, 24,* 3-25.

Eisma, R., Dickinson, A., Goodman, J., Mival, O., Syme, A.,& Tiwari, L.(2003). *Mutual Inspiration in the development of new technology for older people.* Retrieved June 9, 2005, from

http://www.computing.dundee.ac.uk/projects/utopia/publicati
ons/Include2003
Eisma.pdf#search='Mutual%20inspiration%20in%20the%20develop
ment%20of%20new
%20technology%20for%20older%20people'

Ellis, D.,R., Allaire, J. C. (1999).Modeling computer
interest in older adults :The role of age, education,
computer knowledge, and computer anxiety. *Human Factors,*
41, 345-355.

Enders, A. & Spas, D. (2000). *Rates of computer and*
Internet use: A comparison of urban and rural access by
people with disabilities. Retrieved May 27, 2007, from
http://rtc.ruralinstitute.umt.edu/TelCom/computer.htm

E-mail message from Ronald Reazin

E-mail message from Jianling Liu

Emery, V. K., Edwards, P. J., Jacko, J. A., Moloney, K. P.,
Barnard, L., Kongnakorn, T., Sainfort, F., Scott, I. U
(2003,November). *Toward achieving universal usability for*
older adults through multimodal feedback. Paper accepted
for publication in the Proceedings of the 2003 ACM
Conference on Universal Usability (CUU 03), Vancouver, BC,
Canada.

Eysenck, M. W., & Calvo, M.G. (1992). Anxiety and
performance:The processing efficiency theory. *Cognition and*
Emotion, 6, 409-434.

Fajou, S.(n.d.).*Computer Anxiety.* Retrieved July 12, 2006,
from July 12, 2006, from
http://www.edfac.usyd.edu.au/projects/comped/Fajou.html

Finn, J. (n.d.). *Aging and information technology: The*
promise and the challenge. Retrieved May 29, 2006 from
http://www.generationsjournal.org/generations/gen-21-
3/finn.html

Fisk, A. D., Rogers, W. A., Charness, N., Czaja, S.J., &
Sharit, J. (2004).*Designing for older adults: Principles*
and creative human factors approaches. Boca Raton, FL : CRC
Press.

184

Fletcher-Flinn, C.M. and Suddendorf, T. (1996). Computer attitudes, gender and exploratory behavior: A developmental study. *Journal of Educational Computing Research, 15,* 369-392.

Florida State University.(2006).*Office of Institutional Research.* Retrieved May 26 2007, from http://www.ir.fsu.edu/moreinfo.cfm?CAT=reports

Florida State University.(2007).*Office of Institutional Research.* Retrieved September 15, 2007, from http://www.ir.fsu.edu/

Fox,S.(2004).Older Americans and the Internet. Pew Internet & American Life Project. Retrieved from http://www.pewinternet.org/

Friedberg, L. (2001). *The impact of technological change on older workers: Evidence from data on computer use.* Retrieved May 29, 2006, from http://papers.nber.org/papers/w8297.pdf

Frideris, J.S., Goldenberg, S., Disanto, J., & Fleising, U. (2006). *Examples & Cases.* Retrieved May 1, 2004, from http://216.109.125.130/search/cache?ei=UTF-8&p=CAS+%28MArcoulides%2C+1989%3B+Examples+and+cases&fr=yfp-t-405&u=www.ocf.berkeley.edu/%7Ekywong/examplesAndCases.htm&w=cas+marcoulides+1989+examples+example+cases+case&d=IpGzcul jPHFT&icp=1&.intl=us

Fulks, J.S. (n.d.). *Putting a definition to aging—News/reference.* Retrieved March 3, 2005, from http://www.penpages.psu.edu/penpages reference/28507/285072 485.HTML

Garson, G.D. (2007). *Sampling.* Retrieved July 27, 2006, from http://www2.chass.ncsu.edu/garson/pa765/sampling.htm

Gephart, W.J.(1982).Microcomputers in education. *Practical Applications of Research, 4* (4),1-4.

Gietzelt, D. (2001). *Computer and internet use among a group of Sydney seniors:A pilot study.* Retrieved June 20, 2005, from http://www.alia.org.au/publishing/aarl/32.2/full.text/geitz elt.html

Gilroy, F.D. & Desai, H.B. 1986, Computer anxiety: Sex, race, and age. *International Journal of Man-Machine Studies, 25,* 711 – 719.

Glass, C.R. & Knight, L.A.(1988).Cognitive Factors in Computer Anxiety. *Cognitive Therapy and Research, 12,* 351-365.

Gleick, J. (1999).*Faster: The Acceleration of Just About Everything.* New York: Pantheon Books.

Hanson, V, (2001)- *Web access for elderly citizens.* Retrieved August 25, 2005, from ACM database

Henderson, R., Deane, F., Barrelle, K., & Mahar, D. (1995). Computer anxiety: Correlates, norms, and problem definition in health care and banking employees using the Computer Attitude Scale. *Interacting with Computers,* 7, 181-19.

Hargittai, E. (2003). *The digital divide and what to do about it.* Retrieved September 08, 2004, from http://www.eszter.com/papers/co4-digitaldivide.html

Hargrove, T. & Stempel III, G.H. (2002). *The 'digital divide' is shrinking.* Retrieved August 29, 2004, from http://www.seattlepi.nwsource.com/business/82316 netuse.sht ml

Harris, J. B., & Grandgenett, N. (1997).Correlates among teachers' anxiety, demographic, and telecomputing activity. *Journal of Research on Computing in Education, 28,* 300-317.

Hartley, J. (1994). *Designing instructional text.* East Brunswick, New Jersey: Nichols.

Hartley, A.A., Hartley, J.T., & Johnson, S. A. (1996). *Aging and technological advances: The older adult as a computer user.* New York: Plenum.

Havelka, D., Beasley, F., & Broome, T. (2004). A Study of computer anxiety among business students. *Business Education, 19* (1). Retrieved May 27, 2007, from http://www.bsu.edu/mcobwin/majb/?p=128

Hawthorn, D. (2000). Possible implication of aging for interface designers. *Interacting with Computers, 12,*507-528.

Heinssen, R.K., Glass, C.R., & Knight, L.A.(1987). Assessing computer anxiety: Development and validation of the Computer Anxiety Rating Scale. *Computer in Human Behavior,3,* 49-59.

Hill, T., Smith, N.D., & Mann, M.F.(1987).Role of efficacy expectations in predicting the decision to use advanced technologies :The case of computers. *Journal of Applied Psychology, 72,* 307-313.

Hintze, W. & Lehnus, J.(2004).*Media habits and Internet usage among America's youth.* Retrieved August 31, 2003, from http: www.internationalmta.org/1998/9813d.html

Hockey, G. R., Briner, R.B., Tattersall, A.J., & Wiethoff, M. (1989). Assessing the impact of computer workload on operator stress: The role of system controllability. *Ergonomics, 32,* 1401-1418.

Hoffman, A. (2006). *Eight tips for older workers in IT.* Retrieved November 20, 2006, from http://careersat50.monster.com/articles/techie/

Holt, B. J. (2000). Creating senior-friendly web sites. *Issue Brief, 1 (4),* 1-8.

Holt, B.J., & Morrell, R.W. (2002). Guidelines for web site design for older adults: The ultimate influence of cognitive factors. In R.W. Morrell (Ed.), *Older adults, health information, and the World Wide Web,* (pp. 109-132). Mahwah, New Jersey: Erlbaum.

Hopson, S.A. (2001). *Assessing and Coping with Technology Anxiety.* Retrieved May 20, 2007, from http://mathstar.nmsu.edu/educ621/shirley2001.html

Howard, G.S., & Smith, R.D.(1986). Computer anxiety in management: Myth or reality. *Communications of the ACM, 29,* 611-615.

Howard, G.S., Murphy, C. M., & Thomas, G. N.(1986, November). *Computer anxiety considerations for design of introductory computer courses*. Paper presented at the National Meeting of The Decision Sciences Institute, Hawaii.

Howell, D. C. (1998).*Fundamental Statistics for the Behavioral Sciences*. New York: Houghton Mifflin.

Hunt, N., & Tyrrell, S. (2004). *Stratified sampling*. Retrieved August 23, 2006, from http://www.mis.coventry.ac.uk/~nhunt/meths/strati.html

Igbaria, M. & Parasuraman, S.(1989) A path analytic study of individual characteristics, computer anxiety and attitudes toward microcomputers. *Journal of Management*, *15*(3), pp. 373-388.

Inkpen, K., Upitis, R., Klawe, M., Lawry, J., Anderson, A., Ndunda, M., Sedighian, K., Leroux, S., Hsu, D. (1994). We have never forgetful flowers in our garden: Girls' responses to electronic games. *Journal of Computers in Math and Science Teaching, 13,* 383-403.

International Federation of Library Associations and Institutions.(1997).*Older People and the Internet*. Retrieved March 19, 2005, from http://www.ifla.org/IV/ifla63/44pt2.htm

Jackson, L., Ervin, K., Gardner, P. & Schmitt, N. (2001). Gender and the Internet: Women communicating and men searching. *Sex Roles, 44,* 363-379.

Jenson, J. (1999). Girls ex machina: A school-based study of gender, culture and technology. Ph.D. Thesis, Simon Fraser University.

Johnson, R.W., & Wiener, J.M.(2006). A profile of older Americans and their caregivers. Retrieved November 19, 2006, from http://www.urban.org/publications/311284.html

Joiner, R., Brosnan, M., Duffield, J., Gavin, J. & Maras, P.(2007).The relationship between Internet identification, Internet anxiety and Internet use. *Computers in Human Behavior, 23*(3).Retrieved May 27, 2007, from PsychInfo database.

Joncour, N., Sinclair, K.E., & Bailey, M. (1994). *Computer Anxiety, Computer Experience and Self-Efficacy.* Retrieved November 19, 2006, from http://www.aare.edu.au/94pap/joncn94401.txt

Kaye, H.S. (2000). Disability and the digital divide. *Disability Statistics Abstract, 22,* 1-6. Retrieved November 19, 2006, from http://dsc.ucsf.edu/pdf/abstract22.pdf

Kelley, C. L.,& Charness, N. (1995).Issues in older adults to use computers. *Behavior and Information Technology, 14,* 107-120.

Kelley, C.L., Morrell, R.W., Park, D.C., & Mayhorn, C. B.(1999). Predictors of electronic bulletin board system use in older adults. *Educational Gerontology, 25,* 19-35.

Kjeldskov, J.,& Graham, C.(n.d.).*A review of mobile HCI research methods.* Retrieved May 20, 2006, from http://kingkong.cc.gatech.edu:8080/hci-seminar/uploads/1/kjeldskov-graham%20MobileHCI%202003.pdf

Koch, C. (1995). *Is equal computer time fair for girls? A computer culture in a grade 7/8 classroom.* Retrieved June 27,2005, from http://taz.cs.ubc.ca/egems/byAuthor.html

Koohang, A.A. (1989). A study of attitudes toward computers: Anxiety, confidence, liking, and perception of usefulness. *Journal of Research on Computing in Education, 22*(2), 137-150.

Korukonda, A. (2007).Differences that do matter: A dialectic analysis of individual characteristics and personality dimensions contributing to computer anxiety. *Computers in Human Behavior, 23,* 1921-1942.

Kosba, A. (1999).Adapting web Information to disabled and elderly Users. Retrieved March 25, 2005, from http://www.ics.uci.edu/~kobsa/papers/1999-webnet99-kobsa.pdf

Kurniawan, S. & Zaphiris, P.(n.d.).*Research-derived web design guidelines for older people.* Retrieved May 20, 2007, from PsychInfo database.

Kuter, U.,& Yilmaz, C.(2001).*Survey methods: Questionnaires and interviews*. Retrieved May 20, 2006 from http://www.otal.umd.edu/hci-rm/survey.html

Laffey, J., & Musser, D. (1998). Attitudes of preservice teachers about using technology in teaching. *Journal of Technology and Teacher Education*, 6(4), 223-241.

Laguna, K., & Babcock, L.(1997). Computer anxiety in young and older adults: Implications for Human-computer interactions in older populations. *Computers in Human Behavior*, *13*, 317-326.

Lantis, M. & Sulewski, M.(1994). *Overcoming computer anxiety in adult learners*. Retrieved May 20, 2007, from PsychInfo database.

Laux, L., McNally, P., Paciello, M., Vanderheiden, G. (n.d.). *Designing the world wide web for people with disabilities: A user centered design approach*. Retrieved May 20, 2007, from PsychInfo database.

Leigh, A. & Atkinson, R.D.(2001).*Clear thinking on the digital divide*. Retrieved August 26, 2005, from http://www.ndol.org/documents/digital_divide.pdf

Lethen, J.(1996). *Introduction to ANOVA*. Retrieved June 12, 2006,from http://www.stat.tamu.edu/stat30x/notes/node126.html

Lipincott, W. & Wilkins (2003).*Integrating Web-based technology into distance education*. Retrieved August 27, 2007,from http://www.medscape.com/viewarticle/464290_4

Liu, M., Reed, W.M., & Phillips, P.D. (1992). Teacher education students and computers: Gender, major, prior computer experience, occurrence, and anxiety. *Journal of Research on Computing in Education*, *24*(2), 457-467.

Loyd, B.H.& Gressard, C.P.(1984). The effects of sex, age and computer experience on computer attitudes. *AEDS Journal*, *5*, 67-77.

Mahar, D., Hendeson, R., & Deane, F. (1997). The effects of computer anxiety, state anxiety, and computer experience on users' performance of computer based tasks. *Personality and Individual Differences*, *22* (5), 683-692.

Maurer, M.M. & Simonson, M.R. (1993-94). The reduction of computer anxiety: Its relation to relaxation training, previous computer coursework, achievement, and need for cognition. *Journal of Research on Computing in Education, 26*(2), 205-219.

Maki, R. & Maki, W.(2003).Prediction of learning and satisfaction in web-based and lecture courses [Electronic version].*Journal of Educational and Computing Research, 28* (3), 197-213.

Marcoulides, G. A.(1989).Measuring computer anxiety: the computer anxiety scale. *Educational and Psychological Measurement, 49,* 733-739.

McDonald, S., & Stevenson, R.J.(1998). Navigation in hyperspace: an evaluation of the effects of navigational tools and subject matter expertise on browsing and information retrieval in hypertext. *Interacting with Computers, 10,* 129-142.

McIlroy, D., Bunting, B., Tierney, K., & Gordon, M.(2001). The relation of gender and background experience to self reported computing anxieties and cognitions. *Computer Human Behaviour, 17,* 21-33.

Mcilroy, D., Sadler, C., & Boojawon, N.(2007).Computer phobia and computer self-efficacy: Their association with undergraduates' use of computer facilities. *Computers in Human Behavior, 23*(3). Retrieved May 28, 2007, from PsychInfo database.

McInerney, V., McInerney, D. M., & Sinclair, K. E.(1990). *Computer anxiety and student teachers: Interrelationships between computer anxiety, demographic variables, and an intervention strategy.* Paper presented at the Australian Association for Research in Education Annual Conference, Sydney, Australia.

Microsoft Presspass.(1997).*Microsoft, AARP announce alliance to provide technology springboard for older Americans : New study shows extent and patterns of computer usage among older adults.* Retrieved December 3, 2006, from http://www.microsoft.com/presspass/press/1997/Dec97/AARPPr. mspx

Mikulincer, M., Kedem, P., & Paz, D. (1990). Anxiety and Categorization- I: The Structure and Boundaries of Mental Categories. *Personality and Individual Differences*, *11*(8), 805-814.

Millward, P. (2003). The 'grey digital divide': Perception, exclusion and barriers of access to the Internet for older people. *First Monday, 8*, 1-14. Retrieved May 20, 2006, from http://firstmonday.org/issues/issues8 7/millward/

Montag, M., Simonson, M.R., & Maurer, M.M. (1984).*Test administrator's manual for the Standardized Test of Computer Literacy and Computer Anxiety Index*. Ames, Iowa: Instructional Resources Centre, Iowa State University.

Morrell, R.W., Dailey, S.R., & Rousseau, G.K. (2003). Applying research: The NIHSeniorHealth.gov Project. In N. Charness & K.W. Schaie (Ed.),*Impact of technology on successful aging*, (pp.134 -161). New York: Springer Publishing Company.

Morrell, R. W., & Echt, K. V.(1996).Instructional design for older computer users: The influence of cognitive factors. In W. A. Rogers, A. D. Fisk, & N. Walker (Eds.), *Aging and skilled performance: Advances in theory and application*, (pp. 241-265). Mahwah, NJ: Lawrence Erlbaum Associates.

Morrow, D.G., & Leirer, V.O. (1999). Designing medication instructions for older adults. In D.C. Park, R.W. Morrell, & K. Shifren (Eds.), *Processing of medical information in aging patients* (pp.249-266). New Jersey: Erlbaum.

Morell, R.W., Mayhorn, C.B., & Bennett, J.(2002). Older adults online in the Internet century. In R.W. Morrell (Ed.), *Older adults, health information, and the World Wide Web* (pp.43-60). New Jersey: Erlbaum.

Morrell, R.W., Park, D,C., Mayhorn, C.B., & Echt, K.V. (1996).*Effects of computer experience on attitudes toward computers in older adults*. Paper presented at the American Psychological Association Annual Meeting, Toronto, Canada.

Morrow,P.C., Prell, E.R., & McElroy, J.C. (1986).Attitudinal and behavioral correlates of Computer Anxiety. *Psychological Reports*, *59*, 1199-1204.

Moti Nissani's Homepage (2000). *A disabled press*. Retrieved July 29, 2007, from
http://www.is.wayne.edu/mnissani/media/disabled.htm

Murphy, C., Coover, D., & Owen, S. (1989). Development and validation of the computer self-efficacy scale. *Educational and Psychological Measurement, 49*, 893-899.

National Institute on Aging & National Library on Medicine.(2004).*Making your web site senior friendly*. Retrieved May 1, 2005, from
http://usability.gov/checklist.pdf

National Telecommunications and Information Administration. (2002). *A Nation Online: How Americans are expanding their use of the Internet*. Retrieved August 23, 2007, from
http://www.dynamicnet.net/news/articles/a_nation_online.htm

National Telecommunications and Information Administration. (n.d.).*Falling through the Net II: New data on the digital divide*. Retrieved May 26, 2007, from
http://www.ntia.doc.gov/ntiahome/net2/falling.html

National Telecommunications and Information Administration. (2000).*Falling through the Net: Toward digital inclusion*. Retrieved August 26, 2005, from
http://search.ntia.doc.gov/pdf/fttn00.pdf

Necessary, J.R. & Parish, T.S. (1996, Spring). The relationships between computer usage and computer-related attitudes and behaviors. *Education, 116*, 384-386.

Newsom, J.(2007).*Types of scales and levels of measurement*. Retrieved March 3, 2007, from
http://www.upa.pdx.edu/IOA/newsom/pa551/lecture1.htm

Nickell, G., & Pinto, J.(1986). The computer attitude scale. *Computers in Human Behavior. 12*, 301-306.

Northern Ireland Government.(2005).*A digital inclusion strategy for Northern Ireland*. (2002).Retrieved August 24, 2005, from
http://www.cituni.gov.uk/pdfs/digitalinclusionstrategy.pdf

Norris, P.(2001). *Digital Divide: Civic engagement, information poverty and the Internet in democratic societies*. Cambridge: Cambridge University Press.

193

Noyes, J.& Sheard, M.(2003). Designing for older adults-Are they a special group? In Constantine Stephanidis (Ed.), *Universal access in HCI: Inclusive design in the information society*, (pp.877-881). New Jersey: Lawrence Erlbaum Associates.

O Brian, S. (2007).*Disability management: Coping with age-related impairments*. Retrieved May 27, 2007, from http://seniorliving.about.com/b/a/207612.htm
Oetting, E.R. (1983). *Mannual for Oetting Computer Anxiety Scale*. Fort Collins, Co.: Rocky Mountain Behaviourial Science Institute.

Ogozalek, V., Z.(1994). *A comparison of the use of text and multimedia interfaces to provide information to the elderly*. Retrieved October 20, 2000, from http://delivery.acm.org/10.1145/200000/191700/p65-ogozalek.pdf?key1=191700&key2=8628015611&coll=Portal&dl=GUIDE&CFID=52277163&CFTOKEN=90950496

Oregon Health & Science University (2001). *Statistical sampling, estimation, and testing*. Retrieved August 14, 2006, from http://www.ohsu.edu/son/faculty/knafl/teaching/II.sampling.pdf

Orr, L.V.(n.d.).*Computer anxiety*. Retrieved June 17, 2007, from http://www.usm.maine.edu/~com/lindap~1.htm

Otter, M., & Johnson, H. (2000).Lost in hyperspace: Metrics and mental models. *Interacting with Computers 13*, 1-40.

Park, D.C. (1992). Applied cognitive aging research. In F.I.M. Craik & T.A. Salthouse (Eds.), *Handbook of cognition and aging*, (pp.449-493). Mahwah, New Jersey: Erlbaum.

Penner, R.G., Perun, P., & Steuerle, E. (2003). *Letting older workers work*. Retrieved May 29, 2006 from http://www.urban.org/UploadedPDF/310861 retirement no16.pdf

Pew Internet & American Life Project.(2004).*Older Americans and the Internet*. Retrieved June 29, 2006, from http://www.pewinternet.org/PPF/r/117/report display.asp

Price, I. (2000). *Independent Samples t - test*. Retrieved May 24, 2007, from

http://www.une.edu.au/WebStat/unit_materials/c6_common_stat
istical_tests/independent_samples_t.html

Questionnaires vs Interviews (n.d.) Retrieved August 30,
2005, from
http://216.109.125.130/search/cache?p=Questionnaires+vs+Int
erviews&sm=Yahoo%21+Search&toggle=1&ei=UTF-
8&u=employees.csbsju.edu/aolson/NUTR330/research/Questionna
ires.pdf&w=questionnaires+vs+interviews&d=BLKOnGFULiDW&icp=
1&.intl=us

Rada, R.,& Murphy, C. (1992).Searching versus browsing in
hypertext. *Hypermedia, 4* (1), 1-30.

Randall, D. (n.d.). *Elders in the age of information and
technology.* Retrieved May 27, 2006 from
http://www.umm.maine.edu/resources/beharchive/bexstudents/D
rewRandall/drbex310.html

Raub, A. C. (1981). *Correlates of computer anxiety in
college students.* Unpublished doctoral major applied
research project, University of Pennsylvania, Philadelphia,
PA.

Raub, A.C.(1982).Correlates of computer anxiety in college
students. (Doctoral dissertation, University of
Pennsylvania.1982).*Dissertation Abstracts International,
42,* 4775.

Ray N. M., & Minch R. P. (1990). Computer anxiety and
alienation: Towards a definition and parsimonious measure.
Human Factors, 32, 477-491.

Ray, C.M., Sormunen, C., & Harris, T. M. (n.d.). Men's and
women's attitudes toward computer technology: A comparison.
Retrieved July 24, 2007, from
http://216.109.125.130/search/cache?ei=UTF-
8&p=ray%2C+sormunen+%26+harris%2C&fr=yfp-t-
471&u=www.osra.org/itlpj/raysormunenharris.PDF&w=ray+sormun
en+harris&d=RuY-1OdmPnYB&icp=1&.intl=us

Reed, W.M., & Overbaugh, R.C. (1993). The effects of prior
experience and instructional format on teacher education
students' computer anxiety and performance. *Computers in
the Schools, 9*(2/3), 75-89.

Richardson, M., Zorn, T.E., Weaver, K. (n.d.). *Senior's perspectives on the barriers, benefits and negative consequences of learning and using computers*. Retrieved May 20, 2005, from http://www.slis.indiana.edu/faculty/hrosenba/www/1574/pdf/richardson_seniornet.pdf

Rogers, W., Fisk, A.D. (2004).*Psychological Science and Intelligent Home Technology: Supporting Functional independence of Older Adults*. Retrieved March 24, 2005, from APA Online web site: http://www.apa.org/science/psa/sb-rogersprt.html

Rosen, L. D., & Maguire, P. (1990) Myths and realities of computer phobia: A meta-analysis. *Anxiety Research, 3*, 175-191.

Rosen, L.D., Sears, D.C. & Weil, M.M. (1987). Computerphobia. *Behavior Research Methods, Instrumentation, & Computers, 19*, 167-179.

Rosen, L.D., & Weil, M.M.(1992). *Measuring Technophobia, A Manual for the Administration and Scoring of the Computer Anxiety Rating Scale, Computer Thoughts Survey and the General Attitudes towards Computers Scale*. California State University Dominguez Hills, Computerphobia Reduction Program.

Rosen, L.D. & Weil, M.M. (1995). Adult and teenage use of consumer, business, and entertainment technology: Potholes on the information superhighway? *Journal of Consumer Affairs, 29*(1), 55-84.

Rosen, L.D. & Weil, M.M. (1994). Computer availability, computer experience and technophobia among public school teachers. *Computers in Human Behavior, 11*(1), 9-31.

Rotstein, G.(1999). *Elderly learn to compute to not be left behind*. Retrieved May 27, 2005, from http://www.post-gazette.com/regionstate/19991010ComputerAge3.asp

Rubey, T. C.(1999). Profile of computer owners in the 1990s. *Monthly Labor Review*. Retrieved July 22, 2007, from http://www.highbeam.com/doc/1G1-55010248.html

Rubin, R.M. & White-Means, S.I. (2000).*Income Distribution of older Americans. Monthly Labor Review*.

Retrieved August March 3, 2005, from
http://www.bls.gov/opub/mlr/2000/11/art2full.pdf#search='in
come%20distribution%20of%20older%20americans'

Russell, J.N., Hendershot, G.E., LeClere, F., Howie, J., &
Adler, M.(1997).*Trends and differential use of assistive
technology devices: United States, 1994.* Retrieved July 29,
2007,from http://216.109.125.130/search/cache?ei=UTF-
8&p=mobility%2C+vision+and+hearing+impairments+under+45+yea
rs+of+age&fr=yfp-t-
405&u=www.cdc.gov/nchs/data/ad/ad292.pdf&w=mobility+vision+
hearing+impairments+under+45+years+year+age+ages&d=Bcy5Welj
O6xt&icp=1&.intl=us

Salthouse, T. A. (1990). Cognitive competence and expertise
in aging. In J. E. Birren & K. W. Schaie (Eds.), *Handbook
of the psychology of aging* (3rd Ed.), (pp. 310-319). San
Diego: Academic Press.

Sam, H. K., Othman, A. E., Nordin, Z., N. (2005).Computer
self-efficacy, computer anxiety, and attitudes towards the
Internet: A study among undergraduates in Unimus.
Educational Technology & Society, 8, 205-219.Retrieved June
15, 2006 from http://www.ifets.info/journals/8_4/19.pdf

Samorodov, A. (1999).*Aging and labor markets for older
workers.* Retrieved May 29, 2006 from
http://www.ilo.org/public/english/employment/strat/publ/etp
33.htm

Savenye, W.C., Davidson, G.V., & Orr, K.B. (1992). Effects
of an educational computing course on preservice teachers'
attitudes and anxiety toward computers. *Journal of
Computing in Childhood Education,* 3, 31-41.

Schoon, P., & Cafolla, R.(2002).World Wide Web hypertext
linkage patterns. *Journal of Educational Multimedia
Hypermedia, 11*(2), 117-139.

Sharit, J. & Czaja, S.J. (1994), Ageing, computer-based
task performance, and stress: Issues and challenges,
Ergonomics, 37, 559-577.

Shashaani, L.(1997).Gender differences in computer
attitudes and use among college students. *Journal of
Educational Computing Research, 16,* 37-51.

197

Shashaani, L.(1994).Gender-differences in computer experience and its influence on computer attitudes. *Journal of Educational Computing Research, 11*, 347-367.

Shih, P., Munoz, D., & Sanchez, F.(2006). The effect of previous experience with information and communication technologies on performance in a web-based learning program. *Computers in Human Behavior, 22*, 962-970.

Simon, A. (1996).*Consumers and cyberspace: Inequitable distribution of information.* Retrieved August 27, 2006, from http://216.109.125.130/search/cache?ei=UTF-8&p=income+and+computer+anxiety&fr=yfp-t-501&u=hec.osu.edu/people/shanna/cyber/simonaci.htm&w=income+computer+computers+anxiety&d=EAmP1_4-PTB3&icp=1&.intl=us

Smith, B., & Caputi, P. (2007). Computers in Human Behavior, *23* (3), 1481-1498.

Smith, S., & Gove, J.E. (n.d.) *Physical changes of aging.* Retrieved June 23, 2006, from http://edis.ifas.ufl.edu/pdffiles/HE/HE01900.pdf

Smith, M. N., & Kotrlik, J. W. (1990). Computer anxiety among extension agents: A barrier that can be reduced. *Journal of Extension, 28* (4). Retrieved February 1, 2007, from http://www.joe.org/joe/1990winter/ent.html

Spry Foundation.(1999).*Older Adults and the World Wide Web.* Retrieved January 5, 2004, from http://www.spry.org/pdf/website creators guide.pdf

Stapleton, C. (1997). *Basic concepts in exploratory Factor Analysis (EFA) as a tool to evaluate Score Validity: A right-brained approach.* Retrieved January 10, 2004, from http://ericae.net/ft/tamu/Efa.HTM

StatPac. (1997).*Advantages of written questionnaires.* Retrieved June 12, 2006, from http://www.statpac.com/surveys/advantages.htm

StatPac Inc.(1997). *Sampling methods.* Retrieved March 19, 2006 from http://www.statpac.com/surveys/sampling.htm

StatPac Inc. (1997). *Questionnaire Design General Considerations.* Retrieved May 20, 2005, from http://www.statpac.com/surveys/questionnaire-design.htm

StatSoft Inc. (1984). *Basic Statistics.*
Retrieved May 3, 2007, from
http://www.statsoft.com/textbook/stbasic.html

Steinhauser, S.(n.d.). *Beyond age bias: Successfully managing an older workforce.* Retrieved May 29, 2006, from http://clem.mscd.edu/~steinhas/beyond_bias.htm

Steinmetz, E.(2006).*Americans with disabilities:2002.*
Retrieved July 29, 2007, from
http://www.census.gov/hhes/www/disability/sipp/disab02/awd0
2.html

Teel D.S.(2005).*Technology and senior citizens.* Retrieved August 26, 2005, from
http://www.sunliving.com/seniortech.html

Texas A & M University.(n.d.)*Statistics.*
Retrieved July 5, 2007, from
http://www.stat.tamu.edu/spss.php

The University of Arizona. (2007). *Aging: What is aging?.*
Retrieved December 3, 2006, from
http://student.biology.arizona.edu/honors99/group12/what.ht
m

The University of Hawai'i System.(2007).*Sampling strategies and their advantages and disadvantages.* Retrieved July 23, 2006, from
http://www2.hawaii.edu/~cheang/Sampling%20Strategies%20and%
20their%20Advantages%20and%20Disadvantages.htm

The University of Texas at Austin. (n.d.).*SPSS for Windows: Descriptive and Inferential Statistics.* Retrieved July 5, 2007, from
http://www.utexas.edu/its/rc/tutorials/stat/spss/spss2/inde
x.html

Timmerman, S.(1998). The Role of Information Technology in Older Adult Learning. In J. C. Fisher and M. A. Wolf (Eds.), *Learning: Meeting the challenges of older adulthood.* San Francisco, CA: Jossey-Bass.

Todman, J., & Dick, G.(1993).Primary children and teachers' attitudes to computers. *Computers and Education*, 20, 199-203.

Torallba, M. (2000, May) *Magazine: Florida State U. among 'America's Most Wired Colleges'*. Retrieved July 31, 2005, from
http://www.highbeam.com/library/doc0.asp?docid=1P1:26731158&refid=ink tptd np&skeyword=&teaser

Torkzadeh, G. & Angulo, I. E. (1992). The concept and correlates of computer anxiety. *Behaviour & Information Technology, 11* (2), 99-108.

Torkzadeh, G., & Koufterous, X. (1994). Factoral validity of a computer self-efficacy scale and the impact of computer training. *Educational and Psychological Measurement, 54*(3), 813-921.

Trochim, W.M. (2000).*Research Methods Knowledge Base - Survey Research*. Retrieved June 24, 2006,from
http://trochim.human.cornell.edu/kb/survey.htm

Trochim, M.K. (2002). *Reliability*. Retrieved May 3, 2007, from
http://216.109.125.130/search/cache?ei=UTF-8&p=trochim+%282002%29+on+%2Breliability+coefficient&u=www.indiana.edu/%7Eeducy520/sec5982/week 3/rel val trochim.pdf&w=trochim+2002+reliability+coefficient+coefficients&d=QFJSEOdmPalt&icp=1&.intl=us

Trochim, W.(2006).*Construct Validity*. Retrieved June 10, 2006, from
http://www.socialresearchmethods.net/kb/constval.htm

Trochim, W.M. (2006). *Probability sampling*. Retrieved March 22, 2006, from
http://www.socialresearchmethods.net/kb/sampprob.htm

Tulane University. (2007). *Basics of statistical analysis*. Retrieved July 15, 2006, from
http://www.tulane.edu/~panda2/Analysis2/sidebar/stats.htm

UCLA Disability Access Web. (1999). *Specific barriers to web access*. Retrieved June 17, 2006, from
http://www.accessweb.ucla.edu/dis-web.htm

University Minnesota. (2007). *An Overview :Choosing the Correct Statistical Test*. Retrieved may 3, 2007, from http://www-users.cs.umn.edu/~ludford/stat_overview.htm

University of Richmond. (1995). *Sampling techniques*.
Retrieved August 26, 2006 from
http://www.richmond.edu/~sclark3/HSS300/Presentations/HSS30
0 Notes SamplingTechniques.html

University of Washington. (2006). *Access to computers*.
Retrieved November 19, 2006, from
http://www.washington.edu/doit/MathSci/computers.html

U.S. Census Bureau. (2001). *Home computers and Internet use
in the United States: August 2000*. Retrieved July 14, 2005,
from http://www.census.gov/prod/2001pubs/p23-207.pdf

U.S. Department of Commerce. (2002). *A Nation Online*: How
Americans are expanding their use of the Internet.
Retrieved August 28, 2005, from
http://www.ntia.doc.gov/ntiahome/dn/anationonline2.pdf

UW Courses Web Server. (2000). *Psych 218 - Third SPSS
Tutorial Multiple Comparisons*. Retrieved July 5,
2007, from
http://courses.washington.edu/stat217/218tutorial3.html

Van Leeuwe, P. (2006). *Keeping older workers in the work
force: An assessment of recent policies in the Netherlands*.
Retrieved November 23, 2006, from
http://www.cicerofoundation.org/pdf/lecture VanLeeuwe.pdf

Volman, M. (1997). Gender-related effects of computer and
information literacy education. *Journal of Curriculum
Studies*, *29*, 329-349.

Walker, N., Millians, J., & Worden, A. (1996). *Mouse
accelerations and performance of older computer users*.
Paper presented at the Proceedings of the Human Factors and
Ergonomics Society 40th Annual Meeting, Philadelphia.

Westerman, S.J., Davies, D.R., Glendon A.I., Stammers,
R.B., & Matthews, G. (1995). Age and cognitive ability as
predictors of computerized information retrieval. *Behavior
and Information Technology*, *14*, 313-326.

Williamson K., Bow A., & Wale K. (1997). Breaking down the
barriers to public Internet access.' In P. Enslow, P.
Desrochers, & I. Bonifacio (Eds.), *Global Networking 97*,

*proceedings of a joint conference of the international
telecommunications society and international council of
computer communications IOS press* (Vol. 2),(pp.442-449).
Amsterdam.

Wilfong, J.D. (2006). Computer anxiety and anger: the
impact of computer use, computer experience, and self-
efficacy beliefs. *Computers in Human Behavior, 22,* 1001-
1011.

Whitcomb, G. (n.d.).*Computer games for the elderly..*
Retrieved May 20, 2007, from PsychInfo database.
Wolfram Mathworld. (1999).*ANOVA.* Retrieved July 23, 2006,
from http://mathworld.wolfram.com/ANOVA.html

Worden, A., Walker, N., Bharat, K., & Hudson,
S.E.(1997).Making computers easier for older adults to use:
Area cursors and sticky icons. In S. Pemberton (Eds.),
*Proceedings of the ACM CHI 97 Human Factors in Computing
Systems Conference,* (pp. 266-271). Atlanta, Georgia.

Yang, H.H., Mohamed, D., & Beyerbach, B. (1999).An
Investigation of Computer Anxiety Among Vocational-
Technical Teachers. *Journal of Industrial Teacher
Education, 37.* Retrieved May 30, 2006, from
http://scholar.lib.vt.edu/ejournals/JITE/v37n1/yang.html

Yu, C., DiGangi, S.A., Jannasch-Pennell, A., &
Collins, C. (n.d.). Gathering and scattering : A study
of the relationship between mental modeling, physical
modeling and problem solving. Retrieved May 5, 2007,
from http://www.creative-wisdom.com/pub/aera2000.html

Zajicek, M (2001). Supporting older adults at the
interface. In C. Stephanidis (Ed.), Universal Access in
HCI: Towards an information society for all, (pp.454-458).
Mahawah, NJ: Erlbaum.

Zajicek, M. (n.d.).*Interface design for older adults.*
Retrieved May 20, 2007, from PsychInfo database.
Zaphiris, P., & Kurniawan, S. H. (2001). Effects of
information layout on reading speed differences between
paper and monitor presentation. Retrieved May 27, 2006,
from
http://www.soi.city.ac.uk/~zaphiri/Papers/hfes2001_reading.
pdf

BIOGRAPHICAL SKETCH

Bonny Bhattacharjee was born on August 30, 1969, in Calcutta, West Bengal, India. Her father owns a pharmaceutical company in Calcutta, and her mother is a house wife. She has five siblings all younger than her, three sisters and a brother. She also has a brother-in-law and two nieces.

She graduated from M.B. Girls' High School and Hindi High School (Girls' Section) and entered Presidency College, Calcutta, in the year 1988 to pursue a 3-year honors degree in Political Science. Having graduated from Presidency College in 1991, she subsequently earned a Master's degree in Sociology, from the University of Calcutta in the year 1994. From 1993 to 1997 she worked in various capacities in the corporate world. She was also a journalist for a substantial period of time.

As a foreign student in America, she earned a Master's degree in Mass Communications from Murray State University, Kentucky. In the fall of 2001 she joined Florida State University as a Ph.D. student in the College of Information, then referred to as School of Information Studies. She finally received her Ph.D. degree under the direction of Professor Dr. Corinne Jorgensen on October 30, 2007.

www.ingramcontent.com/pod-product-compliance
Lightning Source LLC
Chambersburg PA
CBHW071424050326
40689CB00010B/1966